PRO-LIFE CHAMPION

Msgr. Philip J. Reilly

PRO-LIFE CHAMPION

The Untold Story of Monsignor Philip J. Reilly
and His Helpers of God's Precious Infants

Frederick W. Marks, Ph.D.

Frederick W. Marks

CONTENTS

Acknowledgments vii

Introduction. ix

Chapter 1: The Background 1

Chapter 2: The Man 15

Chapter 3: The Founder 29

Chapter 4: The Victor. 43

Chapter 5: The Tactician. 61

Chapter 6: The Teacher. 77

Chapter 7: The Thinker 95

Chapter 8: The Defendant 117

Chapter 9: The Final Analysis 135

Postscript 151

End Notes 153

APPENDICES

Appendix A: Monsignor's Description of
the Helpers' Mission. 161

Appendix B: The Helpers Handout – Specifics 167

Appendix C: Author's Letter to the Nobel Peace
Prize Committee. 169

Key Dates. 171

Index 179

About the Author. 189

ACKNOWLEDGMENTS

I wish to thank those who cheered me on during the writing of *Pro-Life Champion*, in particular, Kevin Moore, and his wife, Susan; also Florence Maloney, Mother Agnes Mary Donovan, S.V., and Bishop Nicholas DiMarzio. Sr. Mary of the Precious Blood, who has taken care of Monsignor since 1991, unpacked a trunkful of memories for me.

Responsibility for the text as it stands is fully mine, but a number of people offered helpful suggestions after reading the work in manuscript form. They include Rev. Michael Bruno, a professor of history and theology at St. Joseph's Seminary in Dunwoodie, along with Rev. Sean Ogle and Rev. Kevin Sweeney, both of whom knew Monsignor at Cathedral Prep.

Sr. Maria Veritas Marks, O.P. (my daughter) prayed for me, and Rosemary Abruzzino, one of the charter members of the Helpers, had the priests and brothers of the Passionist Community remember me in their Masses.

For all of this I am most grateful. I doubt, however, that I would ever have persevered without the help of Monsignor himself, who granted me seventy hours of interview time, along with unlimited access to his extensive collection of newspaper clippings, legal documentation, and monthly newsletters. It has been my privilege not only to hear him preach on numerous occasions, but also to march with him on dozens of prayer vigils.

As for my wife, Sylvia, there isn't room on a single page to mention all the ways in which she has smoothed the way. Suffice it to say that her patience, tenderness, and technical know-how saved me, on numerous occasions, from sinking into the deep dark blue.

INTRODUCTION

God alone judges souls. But for those who believe that the deliberate taking of innocent human life is gravely sinful, it follows, as night follows day, that ninety-eight percent of the murders committed in the United States are abortions. The gruesomeness of the situation was brought home to me recently when one of my neighbors remarked that "two people go into an abortion mill and one comes out."

In the eyes of Catholics, as well as Muslims (abortion is illegal in every Arab country), killing of the unborn is the ultimate child abuse. An unborn baby is torn to pieces and sucked out. For late-term abortions, the child is often burned to death by replacing the mother's amniotic fluid with a saline solution. And all for profit. Doctors willing to perform abortions can make several hundred thousand dollars a year working part-time for only a few hours a day.

What follows is the story of a man, Monsignor Philip J. Reilly, who has moved mountains to bring this barbaric practice to an end. Nearly every day for the past twenty-seven years he has saved babies by direct, hands-on street counseling while training hundreds of volunteers to do the same. It is estimated that the number of people who owe their lives to his apostolate exceeds a hundred thousand, and this is not to mention the healing effect of his prayer and advocacy on the souls of countless parents bent on destroying God's greatest gift. Hardly a week goes by when a woman doesn't approach him on the street and tell him, "I'm five months pregnant because you were here when I needed encouragement." Or "see this five-month-old boy of mine? He owes his life to you."

Above all, this is the story of a man who has redirected the American pro-life movement from a course of civil disobedience, bombings, and killings to a path of peaceful witness to the sacredness of human life. Police-protected prayer vigils for conversion, mercy, and healing are now the order of the day.

The Helpers of God's Precious Infants, which Reilly founded in 1989, has chapters all over the world, and the work of some of its members is legendary. Take, for example, Dan Goodnow. For the past fourteen years, he has spent six hours a day, five days a week counseling at a brace of abortion mills in Detroit, Michigan, and he claims to have talked approximately 14,000 women out of killing their babies. The figure seems incredible; yet it squares with the fact that Michigan has experienced one of the greatest drop-offs in abortion of any state in the Union.[1]

I'll never forget the time I first witnessed a turnaround. A counselor was able to speak to a young woman as she approached a clinic, and it was clear from the look on her face that she was open to what he was saying. Impassive at first, she grew more and more receptive until, at last, I could tell that a great weight that had been lifted from her shoulders. She seemed grateful and relieved.

The liberating power of truth is beyond telling. Doctors and staff members have been touched by it. Neutral bystanders with nothing whatever to do with abortion have observed the Helpers in action and seen the light. People singing hymns and praying the

Rosary, oftentimes on their knees, are bound to attract attention, for what could be kinder or more compassionate than being present when people – in this case, very young people – are dying?

When Francis Cardinal George, who led twelve hundred Helpers in prayer at a killing mill in Chicago, was asked by reporters to give a reason for what he was doing, he called street witness "a normal pastoral response":

> The Church always accompanies the dying with prayer.
> People die at an abortion clinic. And it is good to pray
> for them and for the living they leave behind. It is also
> good to pray when faced with tragedy. Prayer is an
> appropriate response . . . My decision to participate [in
> the Helpers prayer vigil] was based on the track record of
> the group organizing the event . . . Our society cannot
> indefinitely sustain the playing off of a mother's freedom
> against the death of her child. The country itself will
> eventually come apart. And I was there because no mere
> argument, no matter how well crafted, will convince those
> who sincerely believe in a civil right to abort a baby.

Needless to say, the Cardinal had his critics. But the writer of a *Chicago Sun Times* editorial dated June 26, 1999, was not one of them:

> If the critics of Cardinal Francis George's involvement
> in a peaceful vigil outside of an abortion clinic could
> only hear themselves, they'd be amazed. They sound
> like 1960s bigots and hotheads who screamed that
> the clergy who fought against racism and war should

"go back where they belong – the pulpit. They got
no business coming here, making people angry and
threatening peace . . . " So it was when the Rev. Martin
Luther King, Jr. led a peaceful march in Gage Park. So
it was when busloads of religious people went South
to protest Jim Crow laws. So it was when clergy and
laity concerned here protested the Vietnam War.

So it will be whenever religious leaders challenge the
nation's conscience and make people uncomfortable
by spotlighting in a peaceful, non-violent manner, the
day's great moral conflicts. And there is no greater
moral issue today than abortion – the killing of humans
even after they can live outside the womb, even as they
are emerging from the birth canal . . . the grotesquely
reasoned *Roe v. Wade* decision removed abortion as a
legitimate issue to be resolved by public policy debate.
This left people who believe abortion is a moral evil the
same alternative faced by those in the 1960s who believed
that legalized segregation was a moral evil: go to the
place of the moral evil, and, by our presence, shine the
spotlight on it . . . . Cardinal George and his supporters
had it right. They turned aside insult with the calming,
serene sound of prayer and song. With no slogans or
signs, they reached inside for something stronger than
the insults hurled against them. They committed an
act of faith and love that, if nourished, can blossom
into a social movement that can enlighten this land,
just as the abolitionist and suffrage movements did.

In subsequent chapters, we will focus on the uniqueness of Monsignor's peaceful, non-confrontational approach to pro-life witness and show how it changed the course of history. He spends three to six hours Tuesday through Saturday in anti-abortion activity on the streets of Brooklyn, the most pro-abort borough of the most pro-abort city of the most pro-abort state of the most pro-abort country in the world. He has been shoved. He has had things thrown at him. He has been sued for over a million dollars. His life has been threatened.

Psychologically, he manages to hold his own, but the price in physical terms has been high. Prolonged exposure to the sun resulted in a severe case of skin cancer. Most of his nose had to go. Fifty stitches were required to remove a neck tumor, and skin grafts from the rest of his body were needed to patch his forehead and ears. There were times when he went down to the abortuary with bandages all over his face, and he's not yet out of the woods. In spite of thirty-two radiation treatments and forty hours of hyperbaric oxygen therapy, his "thorn in the flesh" remains.

They say that God loves a cheerful giver. If so, He must be fond of Monsignor for the way he jokes about leaving his nose in the trunk of his car, a twenty-seven-year-old Buick. The other day, after rolling down one of his car windows to let in some air, I tried rolling it back up, and it wouldn't budge. "Don't worry," he said, "every time I start the car, it goes back up a bit. The beauty of owning a clunker is that no one will steal it." He should know. He has parked in some pretty God-forsaken places.

At the Monastery of the Precious Blood in Brooklyn, where he serves as chaplain, rust clings to the gates of his car park. Weeds grow luxuriantly along the driveway. Paint peels on the wall leading up to his second-story bedroom. Apart from the Roman collar that he wears morning, noon, and night, he is partial only to a pair of well-worn running shoes.

We shall have more to say about Monsignor's character and the events that brought him to the championship of the unborn. But first, a word about how his pro-life campaign fits into the overall historical context.

CHAPTER 1

THE BACKGROUND

Respect for human life, as we know it, began thousands of years ago when the Jews recognized that mankind, made in the image and likeness of God, is sacred. If human life is sacred, then the act that produces it is sacred as well, along with the institution that protects it (marriage). Child sacrifice, sterilization, fornication, adultery, sodomy – all were severely punished under the Mosaic law. Severance of the marriage bond was permitted, but not approved, because God, in the words of the prophet Malachi, "hates" divorce.[1]

This is not to deny that child sacrifice figures in the history of the Israelites. Children were offered to the god, Moloch, and thrown into the fire. Excavations in the valley of Gehenna outside Jerusalem have revealed piles of ashes and vestiges of infant skeletons in cemeteries around heathen altars. Such practice was regarded as scandalous, however, by those who took their faith seriously. Moses banned it, Jeremiah and Ezekiel condemned it, the best Jewish kings did what they could to root it out.

Jesus, who used the name Gehenna as a synonym for hell, raised the bar still higher by equating lustful looks with adultery and banning remarriage after divorce.[2] His cousin, John, gave his life as a witness to the immorality of Herod's union with his brother's wife.[3]

Centuries later, when Christianity became the dominant religion of the Roman Empire, child sacrifice was eliminated. Deformed babies were no longer left on the street to die, and by the dawn of the Renaissance, there was hardly a European alive who doubted the sacredness of human life. Christopher Columbus, on reaching San Salvador, was horrified to find that the remnant of a tribe had been eaten alive by its neighbors, the Caribs. When Pizarro reached Peru, he, too, was revolted. The Incas had just flung the bodies of some 20,000 members of a rival tribe into a lake.

In Mexico, the Aztec empire, which was one of the world's cruelest, required a thousand human "sacrifices" annually from every town with a temple. There were 371 subject towns, and the number of killings on a yearly basis is said to have been in the vicinity of 50,000. The early Mexican historian Ixtilzochitl estimated that one out of every five children in Mexico died this way. According to Professor Warren Carroll, entire tribes numbering in the tens of thousands were exterminated by sacrifice: "The most feared and evil leader in the later days of the empire was Tlacaellel, who, on the occasion of dedicating a new pyramid-temple in 1487, sacrificed between 20,000 and 80,000 men in a period of four days."[4]

Not all the conquistadores were virtuous. But there can be little doubt that indignation over the mass killing of defenseless innocents was one of the motives for Spanish colonization.

The first grave undermining of respect for life in Western Europe came when Protestant leaders, following the example of the schismatic Eastern Orthodox Churches, allowed remarriage after divorce. Next came the acceptance of artificial contraception at the Lambeth Conference of Anglicans in 1930. Based on the assumption that the unitive and procreative functions of sex are separate and distinct, Lambeth proved devastating to the culture of life. Marital relations would soon be widely regarded as a recreational activity, promiscuity would skyrocket, and abortion, along with sodomy, would gain acceptance because evil is not good at calling out evil.

Pope Pius XI's answer to Lambeth was *Casti Connubii* (1930), a powerful encyclical reaffirming the Catholic ban on artificial contraception. A half century later, Pope Paul VI came out with *Humanae Vitae* (1968), highlighting the sacredness of human life, along with the act that produces it. Henceforth, there could be no doubt whatever about the Church's teaching on artificial contraception – i.e. that such practice, before or during the marital act, is intrinsically evil. There were critics who refused to accept the infallibility of *Humanae Vitae*, but they were on shaky ground since the author of the encyclical made no less than three references to his Petrine teaching authority.

The successors of St. Peter, by coming down unequivocally on the side of Christian tradition and the Natural Law, had done their duty. But the reaction to *Humanae Vitae* in much of the developed, industrial world was disappointing in the extreme. A huge majority of the "faithful" continued to practice contraception in defiance of papal teaching, and this, added to media propaganda proclaiming the supremacy of the individual conscience over the dogma of the Magisterium, threw the American Church into chaos. Abortion was embraced nationwide as a necessary backup measure for contraceptive failure. Legalization came in 1973 with *Roe v. Wade* followed in 2015 by a second legalization – that of "same-sex marriage" (*Obergefell v. Hodges*). Suddenly, it was fashionable to attack the rights of conscience. Taxpayers were forced to underwrite abortion, and sex education was mandated for schools.

The rate of killing that followed *Roe v. Wade* – fifty million children slaughtered in fifty years -- beggars the imagination. In the Bronx, more babies were aborted than born during a year for which we have reliable statistics (1997-98), with the rate for blacks, who could have voted had their lives been spared, three times greater than that for whites. Ten years later, the picture was unchanged. According to New York State Vital Statistics, seventy out of a hundred black unborn babies perished that year, and eight out of ten of the killings were paid for by the government -- i.e. by taxpayers like you and me.

Much has happened since the days of Hernán Cortes. We have gone from revulsion in the face of child sacrifice to public acceptance. When Mainland China coerced parents into murdering every child that came along after the first -- Chinese leaders have admitted to 400,000,000 forced abortions -- the West did nothing. Congress voted trade sanctions against apartheid in South Africa, but in response to a policy more barbaric and cruel than anything in all the annals of mankind – far more evil than the worst form of social discrimination – American leaders remained mum for the most part.

It would have been unthinkable fifty years ago for anyone to distribute condoms to schoolchildren; equally unthinkable for prime-time TV to portray adultery as a laughing matter, or for judges to legalize abortion on demand. Today, it is the *outlawing* of such things that is unthinkable. Gonorrhea, which had practically died out prior to the modern age, has become the most common infectious disease outside of the flu. Professor Peter Singer of Princeton University, one of America's most prestigous educational institutions, is an unabashed defender of infanticide.

The picture, in short, is dark -- eerily so. What is amazing, though, is that, in spite of all the ground that has been lost, there have been spectacular gains for the anti-abortion movement. Over the past thirty years, two out of every three abortuaries in the nation have closed. Several rulings by the Supreme Court have upheld the right of sidewalk counselors to approach women at the entrance of an abortion clinic, and on the state level, there have been additional victories. On September 6, 1994, the U. S. Court of Appeals for the Second District covering New York struck down, as unconstitutional, arbitrary buffer zones outside abortion clinics.

Why pro-lifers protesting abortion have been so consistently successful in confronting the culture of death is a question we shall attempt to answer. But before doing so, we need to be clear about what makes the work of Monsignor's Helpers so vitally important.

FIGHTING FOR TRUTH

In the first place, they are fighting for truth of the kind that John the Evangelist tells us is necessary if we are to remain free.[5] Satan is the father of lies (John 8:44), and it is clear that abortionists are his minions because, day in and day out, they accuse Monsignor of "harassment." Is it harassment to conduct peaceful, prayerful vigils outside clinics and offer practical alternatives to murder? The nation's #1 baby-killer, Bernard Nathanson, who was responsible for over 60,000 abortions, admitted, after his conversion, that he deliberately over-reported the number of illegal abortions.[6] Still another example of duplicity on the part of pro-aborts: they are in constant denial when it comes to scientific research linking abortion with infertility, suicide, breast cancer, and failure to bond with future children.[7] Routinely, they palm off their procedures as a solution to women's problems when, in reality, they are the cause of physical and psychological ills far worse than any they could possibly alleviate.

One can go further. The executive director of the National Coalition of Abortion Providers said he was conscience-bound to admit that he had lied about the rationale for partial birth abortion in which the child's brain is sucked out and skull collapsed.[8]

Finally, in the two cases which legalized abortion nationwide – *Roe v. Wade* and *Doe v. Bolton* – the plaintiffs, Norma McCorvey and Sandra Cano, admitted not only that they had been lied to, but also that they themselves had lied. One of them claimed to have been the victim of a gang rape that never occurred. The other claimed to be pregnant when she wasn't.[9] Here, as an aside, is McCorvey's description of conditions at one of the mills where she worked:

> Light fixtures and plaster falling from the ceiling; rat
> droppings over the sinks; backed up sinks; and blood
> spattered on the walls. But the most distressing room in
> the facility was the "parts room." Aborted babies were
> stored here. There were dead babies and baby parts
> stacked like cordwood. Some of the babies made it into

buckets and others did not, and because of its disgusting features, no one ever cleaned the room. The stench was horrible. Plastic bags full of baby parts swimming in blood were tied up, stored in the room, and picked up once a week. At another clinic, the dead babies were kept in a big white freezer full of dozens of jars, all full of baby parts, with little tiny hands and feet visible through the jars frozen in blood. The abortion clinic's personnel always referred to these dismembered babies as "tissue."[10]

THE FUTURE OF OUR COUNTRY

A second reason why the work of the Helpers is crucial for the future of America (besides fighting for the truth) may be simply stated: it militates against promiscuity, a major cause of societal decay. Anyone familiar with the rise and fall of civilizations knows what sexual license can do to a people. I. D. Unwin, Oxford University don and the author of *Sex and Culture*, and Pitirim Sorokin, who published *The American Sex Revolution*, have shown, after surveying the history of the world's greatest empires and nation states, that cultural achievement is proportional to the degree of premarital abstinence from sex. Siegfried Ernst, a German physician, explains why in his book *Man the Greatest of Miracles*: "Discipline gives a person more hope and freedom than libertarianism in the long run."[11]

Monsignor's campaign has the added value of acting as a drawing card for non-Catholics, which is a third reason to support it. Eastern Orthodox priests, after marching with Monsignor in Brooklyn, have gone on to lead Helpers prayer vigils in both the Czech Republic and

Russia.[12] An address that Reilly gave while in Latvia was broadcast on Baptist radio. Arriving in the city of Pecs in southern Hungary to lead 300 Catholics on a prayer vigil, he was joined by priests and believers of the Reformed and Lutheran Churches.

On a wider scale, one can see that what applies to the Helpers, in particular, applies to Catholicism in general. Many who convert to the Church of Rome do so out of admiration for its unyielding stance on the life issues. Out of hundreds of thousands of pro-lifers who march every year in Washington, D.C. on the anniversary of *Roe v. Wade*, ninety-five percent are Catholic. But along with Catholic banners, you will see "Lutherans for Life" and "Anglicans for Life."

It is the same with birth control. Paul VI's reaffirmation of the traditional Christian stance on contraception was cheered by a broad spectrum of conservative Protestants, some of whom did more than cheer. For Presbyterian minister Scott Hahn and his wife, Kimberly, *Humanae Vitae* was a come-on to conversion. Dr. Ernst, another seeker who crossed the Tiber (from Lutheranism) described Paul VI as "the last moral bulwark and spiritual authority remaining in the modern world . . . [He has] not yet capitulated to the golden calf . . . When he chose the cross, instead of an easier way, the credibility of the papacy was restored . . . . Probably no other papal decision in history has helped so much to cancel the old mistrust against the papacy."[13]

It so happens that Ernst was the leader of four hundred German physicians who offered Pope Paul state-of-the-art data shoring up the Catholic position, and today, two of his daughters are running Helpers' units -- one in Germany where prayer vigils are conducted in twenty-four cities under the inspired leadership of Wolfgang Hering, the other in Italy where the number of chapters is even higher.

A fourth and final reason why the Helpers' battle against child-killing deserves recognition is its potential to revitalize Catholic leadership in the United States. Unity among the bishops is a necessary first step toward spiritual renewal, and the hope is that with consensus on abortion, which is a matter of life and death, episcopal conferees will be more outspoken on other issues such as cohabitation, contraception, and ex-communication – issues that are equally important, but less clear-cut and more highly contested. It will take time. But as Rev. Terence Henry, TOR, past president of Franciscan University, remarked, "the age of casual Catholicism is over. The age of heroic Catholicism has begun."

MANY HEROES

Heroes in any war are few and far between. But in the battle waged since 1973 to defend the rights of the unborn there have been many, and so it would seem fitting at this point to salute a few of those, who, along with Monsignor Reilly, have labored hard and long in the vineyard of the Lord.

The late Paul Marx, O.S.B. was without compare when it came to publicizing the effects of abortion and contraception. A Benedictine priest who travelled over three million miles and visited all fifty states, along with ninety-one foreign countries, he founded an organization, Human Life International (HLI), that has shipped massive amounts of educational material and sponsored scores of congresses. He also wrote thirteen books, including *The Death Peddlers*, which sold over a million copies. His founding of the Life Center at St. John's College in Collegeville, Minnesota, along with his support for *Humanae Vitae*, cost him his job; and like Monsignor Reilly, he was sued by Planned Parenthood.

Second on a short list of pro-life heroes and heroines would be Judie Brown, president of the American Life League (ALL). In addition to writing twelve books and hosting forums for EWTN, she has spoken on numerous talk shows and appeared on TV programs such as *Oprah*, *The O'Reilly Factor*, *Good Morning America*, and *Larry King Live*. ALL is outstanding, not only for its informational role, but also for its refusal to countenance abortion in cases of rape and incest.

A third headline maker is Joe Scheidler, founder of Chicago's Pro-Life Action League in 1980. Starting as a specialist in picketing, he quickly became an expert on every conceivable method of shutting down abortion clinics. Along the way, his home was vandalized. He was struck and spat upon. His sight was damaged. On the receiving end of innumerable crank calls and death threats, his tires were slashed, his office windows were smashed, and his office was painted with roofing tar.[14]

In 1995, Scheidler published *Closed: 99 Ways to Stop Abortion*, and since then, in addition to producing films on sidewalk counseling and videos featuring former abortionists, he has appeared on numerous TV programs, including *ABC News*, *Nightline*, *Donohue*, *Crossfire*, *Face the Nation*, *Good Morning America*, *MacNeil/Lehrer Report*, and *The O'Reilly Factor*. As a writer, his columns have appeared in newspapers such as *USA Today* and *The Wanderer*, and he has mounted the rostrum in more than a thousand towns, all the while producing a Catholic radio show. When the officers of the National Organization of Women (NOW) sued him in 1986, he fought them all the way to the Supreme Court, and when they refused to accept a 2003 decision in his favor, he kept on fighting until he finally emerged victorious in 2006.

To recognize everyone who played a leading role in the fight against abortion would be impossible. However, there are two names, yet to be mentioned, that stand at the very top of the honor roll: those of Randall Terry and Joan Andrews.

Terry first. As the founder of Operation Rescue in 1986 and its leader for four years, he orchestrated hundreds of attempts to block clinic entrances and disable abortion machinery. He was not the first to organize rescues, but the scale on which he planned and carried them out was unprecedented, as was the publicity they achieved.

Joan Andrews Bell, the best-known rescuer of all time, was taken into custody over two hundred times. When she refused to cooperate with prison authorities in Florida as a protest against unjust detention, she was forced to undergo months of solitary confinement, along with a humiliating strip search in the presence of a male prison guard. Her campaign became a *cause célèbre*, attracting the support of such pro-life luminaries as Fr. Marx, Judie Brown, Bernard Nathanson (soon to be her godson), Joe Scheidler, Methodist minister Donald Wildmon, and Chuck Colson, an evangelical convert to Christianity. Over two thousand letters demanding her release by pardon, commutation, or clemency rained down on the desk of Governor Robert Martinez.

No one can ever take away from Joan and fellow rescuers like John Ryan (who was arrested 400 times), the credit owed to them for what they suffered. But, as we will see in a later chapter, the backlash generated by their civil disobedience mounted to the point where they, along with other followers of Randall Terry, were faced with determined resistance on Capitol Hill. At the same time, the controversy engendered by their tactics split the pro-life movement down the middle, making it far less effective than it might otherwise have been. A house divided against itself cannot stand.

The question of whether to push for a constitutional amendment giving states the right to make the final decision on abortion was another source of discord. Such an amendment was proposed by Senator Orin Hatch of Utah in 1981, and some, including Judie Brown, saw it as a weak-kneed compromise.

There was even disagreement on the issue of whether condemnation of abortion should be yoked with opposition to contraception. Those who thought it shouldn't could point to the fact that a large majority of Catholics were contracepting.

WHAT MAKES THE HELPERS UNIQUE

Most pro-life organizations are obliged, by their very nature, to take controversial stands, but the Helpers are blissfully free in this regard. One of their greatest strengths is the fact that they have never been torn from within. In particular, they have never been divided on the issue of civil disobedience since their very existence hinges on the cooperation of law enforcement officers.

While Monsignor hews to the teaching of the Magisterium, following wherever this leads, his mission is not ideological. He is not expected to take a stand on any issue other than the right to life, and who can object to direct, non-confrontational intervention to save lives and souls?

Also in favor of the Helpers is their all-volunteer status. None of them draws a salary. During the early years, Sr. Dorothy Rothar, C.S.J., who taught the Helpers method in the United States, as well as abroad, was an exception. She received financial compensation. Monsignor paid her religious order a modest sum to cover expenses. But she eventually formed her own organization, Bright Dawn Ministry.

The executive directors of the American Life League and Priests for Life make a living from what they take in, and the same is true for Human Life International. Not so with Monsignor Reilly. When board members remind him that he's running out of money, his answer is always: "God will provide." Highly sought-after as a speaker, he nevertheless refuses honorariums, and when people ask what he wants for a talk, he tells them, "Nothing. You're going to pay for this after I leave!" (i.e. by joining the Helpers). When he travels, he generally stays with friends or members of the clergy, and if his expenses are not underwritten by the host, he dips into his own pocket – i.e. his pension, social security, or chaplain's stipend.

This is not to say that there's never been any fund-raising. In 1997, the Helpers sponsored a Celebration of Life concert. It featured the internationally acclaimed singer, Dana, who had performed for the Pope. Monsignor invited her to sing at a number of his vigils, and she did. There have also been Christmas solicitations. But all of this is on a relatively small scale – the Helpers have only about a hundred annual contributors. There are no ads in Catholic papers, and Monsignor sees to it that all donations are applied to the needs of mothers who choose life. Approximately 80% of what the Helpers take in is spent on food, clothing, rent, and baby showers for parents who keep their children. The 20% that remains pays for cassettes, videos, postage, and printing. In one year alone, 75,000 fliers were handed out to people approaching the abortion mills.

Like their founder, the Helpers are extraordinarily hardy. Many of them serve until they succumb to spells of dizziness or suffer a loss of faculties. While wind-driven rain bears down on them in spring, blistering heat is their portion in summer and bone-chilling cold in winter. No matter. Maligned by the secular press and ignored or written off as visionary by many in the priesthood, they soldier on, secure in the conviction that a single baby's life and the soul of the parent are worth any sacrifice.

No one who bears witness to the fullness of the truth is going to please the world. When Jerome Lejeune, the French geneticist who discovered the cause of Down Syndrome, questioned the morality of abortion in an address to his scientific colleagues, the audience was scandalized. In a letter written after he finished speaking, he told his wife: "Today I lost my Nobel Prize in medicine." Just so. When the Helpers hit the street, they are ready for whatever comes their way. Whether it be smiles or jeers, they live up to the motto Monsignor has chosen for them: "Neither concerned about praise nor affected by fear."

CHAPTER 2

THE MAN

Born on June 21, 1934, in Maspeth, Queens, Monsignor was baptized at St. Stanislaus Kostka Church and enrolled in the parish school. His Irish-born father, who worked as a guard at Western Electric, hailed from a family of thirteen children, while his American-born mother was the last of ten.

Every week, the Reillys attended Mass with their brood of six; every day they prayed the Rosary. When Philip's four sisters -- his "four mothers," as he calls them -- reached a marriageable age and suitors came calling, the young men were expected to join in family devotions. On such occasions, Mrs. Reilly, who knew many litanies by heart, was not above adding one or two at the end of evening prayer to test the mettle of her prospective sons-in-law. As for Mr. Reilly, he attended three Masses daily after retirement and said a rosary for each of his offspring.

Small wonder that Philip aspired, from the age of seven, to be a priest. The first step, or course, was to become an altar boy. But because he was rather short and looked young for his age, the pastor put him off by requiring memorization of the Latin responses. This, however, did not stop the Reilly boy. He was soon back in the sacristy announcing proudly that he knew all his Latin!

Philip's first day on the altar was far from promising. The priest had no cassock short enough to fit him, and he dropped a huge Mass missal, along with its brass stand, on the polished marble floor. Candle lighting was another challenge because the wicks were way over his head. He couldn't see what he was doing, and the older boys, looking on from afar, rolled in laughter as he tried again and again to get a flame going. His mother, less amused, flew from her pew to the sacristy: "Why isn't someone else taking care of it?" she demanded. A vocation was in the making, and she was not about to brook any interference.

As the years passed and his peers began dating, Philip held back. But it was not because he disliked girls. He liked them a lot. Never for a moment did he doubt that he would make a good husband and father. The girls, for their part, were attracted to the handsome 6'1" basketball star. As the leading scorer on his high school team (and later on a college squad that would win two consecutive championships), he had plenty of admirers. His sisters kept asking him if he knew how many young ladies were lined up for him. Yes, he knew. But he also knew where he was headed, and he hated to lead anyone on. It was an extended family of the kind that belonged to Christ that he wanted. And so it was that after graduating from St. Stanislaus, and then from Cathedral Prep in Brooklyn, he began studies at Immaculate Conception Seminary in Huntington and was ordained a priest in 1960, the year set aside by Pope John XXIII to celebrate the example of St. John Vianney, one of the Church's greatest pastors.

CHAMPION OF THE UNDERDOG

Monsignor has always had an affinity for the underdog, whether it be an unwanted child or a person of color, and running true to form as a seminarian, he chose a service project in an African-American neighborhood. If a child needed baptism, Holy Communion, or Confirmation, he would instruct the whole family, and when, at the end of the project, a special Mass was offered for his pupils, he arranged for the seminary choir to come and sing. People who attended the reception following his first Mass must have wondered why there were two tables of blacks, all of them friends of Fr. Reilly. His eleven-year-old brother, as surprised as anyone, said to him, "You never told me we had black relatives!"

The irony is that, after expressing a willingness to serve in the inner city following ordination, he was assigned to St. Thomas More Parish in Breezy Point, Queens. St. Thomas More was an all-white, gated community. When some black youths came on foot to its beach, they were carted away in a garbage truck. Reilly, furious at the goings on, vowed that he would never swim there again, and he never did. Later, after ingratiating himself with the parishioners, he delivered a homily on the subject of race. But because most members of the parish claimed to be renters without a voice in how the property was managed, his main contribution to Thomas More was an athletic program that made optimal use of its new gymnasium. When a hurricane hit New York and some of the older parishioners were trapped in flood water, the young curate helped with rescue operations. This, however, was the extent of his service. He soon received word that he had been transferred to St. Teresa's parish in South Ozone Park. The pastor at Breezy Point was sorry to see him go. But the next five years were to be extremely fruitful.

ST. TERESA'S

"Father P.J.," as he was called at St. Teresa's, took charge of after-school athletics. Some of the boys were good enough at basketball to make it to the professional ranks, and when they saw him walk onto the court in his long, black cassock, one of them thought he'd have some fun. Unaware of Reilly's high school record, he heaved the ball at him with such force that it nearly knocked him down, hollering, "Do you know what this is for, you in the black dress?" It didn't take long for the man in black dress to show what he could do. After sinking twenty-one consecutive foul shots, he threw the ball back to Mr. Wise Guy -- as fast as it had come.

There was no further trouble with any of the athletes, and, as time passed, Reilly began laying down requirements for continued participation in after-school sports. Weekly Mass attendance was one of them, and those released from public school on Wednesday afternoons for religious instruction had to attend CCD. Bible study took place on Sunday mornings, with classes taught by twenty-five lay catechists who had studied with Father for three hours every Wednesday evening (two years on the Old Testament, two years on the New). In a word, it was spiritual "pay to play."

Catholic war veterans, who normally played cards and drank beer, were told: "You are soldiers. I'm going to make you soldiers of

Christ. What I'd like you to do is go out and start ringing doorbells to find out which people are interested in learning more about the Faith. When we know who they are, we'll begin teaching them." He divvied up the streets to ensure that everyone had a piece of the action, and if any of the residents expressed interest, they were offered three hours of instruction weekly on a day that was mutually convenient.

Students with an extracurricular interest in journalism were reminded that visiting the elderly was one of the corporal works of mercy. Reilly assured them that if they did it, they could get scoops for their paper by inviting seniors to reminisce, while they, for their part, could share stories about happenings at school. It worked like a charm.

Father didn't think much of the standard school dances at which teenagers "hung all over each other." So he buttonholed the hoods who were proud of the fact that they could get the younger ones to do their bidding: "You think the juniors will do whatever you say?" he asked them. "Yes," they replied. "OK. I'll tell you what. Suppose you invite them to a square dance." "Square dance?" they asked. "That's impossible . . . . stupid!" "I know, I know," said Reilly, "that's why I'm suggesting it. You said you can make them do whatever you want. Let's see if you're telling the truth." Long story short: the big shots rose to Reilly's challenge and it wasn't long before signs appeared along the school corridors: "TAKE A DARE, BE A SQUARE."

Although square dancing for young people was anything but mainstream at the time, attendance was excellent, and so was the spirit. Father had told them beforehand: "I want every one of you to do a real square dance and change partners. Yes, I said change partners! Let me see the Virginia Reel done as only young people can do it." The couple who ran the affair turned out to be terrific leaders, and everyone had a grand time learning the steps, dancing to the point of exhaustion, and wanting to know, after the last "Do Si Do," when the next square dance would be held. Eventually, word got out to the adults, and they wanted one, too!

CATHEDRAL PREP

In short, Father set St. Teresa's on fire. Three parishioners, Rosemary Albruzzino, John Collins, and his wife Adelaide, were so moved by what they saw that they were among the first to join the Helpers of God's Precious Infants some thirty years later.

If the folks who called him "Fr. P.J." had any say in it, he would never have left St. Teresa's. But the bishop had other plans. Aware of Reilly's rapport with youth, he transferred him to Cathedral Prep, his alma mater, and it was there, beginning in 1965, that he would spend the next twenty-six years, teaching Latin, running the chess club, and serving as principal. Along the way, in addition to earning advanced degrees in philosophy, theology, and classics, he became a monsignor in 1986 and helped his sister, Frances, who was widowed at the age of forty. He spent time with her seven mostly small children, playing with them and taking them on vacation; and to this day, he remains a positive male influence on his nieces and nephews.

During his years at Cathedral, he also served on an international commission dealing with English in the Liturgy and threw himself into a variety of charitable causes, including Bread for the World, Catholic Relief Services, and leadership programs for minority students. In addition, he coordinated the teaching of Natural Family Planning, started the Naim group for widows and widowers, and enlisted in a cause that would turn his life upside down.

In 1960, the year of his ordination, the contraceptive pill was distributed under the cover of being a health product for the correction of irregular menstrual cycles. Five years later, in 1965, the year of his transferal to Cathedral, the Supreme Court, in *Griswold v. Connecticut*, legalized unrestricted use of the pill by married couples. Both of these events were milestones along his path to pro-life championship because he could see that unless the right to life was protected, all others would be meaningless.

Griswold, in concert with what the Anglican Church had decided at Lambeth, altered the thinking of many Americans, Catholics included, about the purpose of sex. Pregnancy, previously welcomed as a gift to be cherished, came to be feared and avoided at all costs. The Pill, in particular, led to a huge increase in promiscuity, which, in turn, led to the killing fields. Whenever man acts as the arbiter, rather than the steward, of creation, it opens the door to distortions of every kind, including unnatural acts and laboratory reproduction -- a seismic shift.

Another milestone event occurred in 1965 when Paul VI spoke before the United Nations General Assembly. Because his theme, announced in advance, was "no more war," he was treated as a conquering hero. The first two-thirds of his address was interrupted again and again by applause. But to the surprise of many who expected change in the Catholic position on contraception, he went on to say that "the life of man is sacred; no one may dare offend it. Respect for life, even with regard to the great problem of the birth rate, must find here in your Assembly its highest affirmation and its most reasoned defense. You must strive to multiply bread so that it suffices for the tables of mankind, and not rather favor an artificial control of birth, which would be irrational in order to diminish the number of guests at the banquet of life." Silence fell over the hall, and by evening, the mainline media had turned savage.

By 1967, three years before New York became the third state to legalize the killing of the unborn, Fr. Reilly could read the writing on the wall. He wrote a forceful letter to the speaker of the New York Assembly and organized street demonstrations. All in vain. Eventually, abortion was legalized. But he and his confreres refused to give up, and two years later, the state legislature approved a bill making abortion illegal once again. Lt. Governor Malcolm Wilson, a Catholic, could have signed it in the absence of Governor Rockefeller. But he didn't. And when Rockefeller returned to Albany, he vetoed it. Later, when Wilson ran for governor on a pro-life platform, his pro-choice opponent, Hugh Carey, scored points by calling him a phony for his failure to act on conviction.

A thunderbolt had struck. New York's law, the most liberal in the world, allowed abortion up to seven months of pregnancy, and women from all over the world began flocking to the Big Apple. Then came a second bolt from the blue: the Supreme Court's *Roe v. Wade* decision (1973) which not only legalized abortion on demand nationwide, but also invited federal funding.

The Latin teacher whose career we have been following was shocked. Seeing around him a self-destructing world bereft of wisdom, he knew he could not sit back and do nothing. And so, after recruiting seminarians for monthly all-night prayer vigils, he started withholding a portion of his federal taxes, hoping to encourage others to do the same – "priming the pump," as he put it.

A letter that he wrote to a regional head of the IRS made it to the front page of the *Tablet*, the newspaper of the Brooklyn Diocese. But few of his coreligionists followed suit, and IRS "overdue" notices began piling up on his desk. It looked as if he might be off the hook when the Illinois Congressman Henry Hyde passed an amendment to an appropriations bill in 1976 that prohibited the use of taxpayer money for abortion, except in cases of rape, incest, or danger to the life of the mother. There was only one problem. Four hours after the bill's passage, a court-ordered injunction rendered it null and void pending a test of its constitutionality in court.

Larry Washburne, a Wall Street lawyer, took up the cudgels for the Hyde Amendment in a campaign that wound up costing him his job and his home. At the federal courthouse in Brooklyn where Reilly was called as the first witness, Washburne argued that since abortion, as a procedure, was elective, rather than necessary, it was not a constitutional right; hence taxpayers should not have to pay for it. Months became years. But in the end, Reilly, whose tax form went all the way to the Supreme Court, never had to pay his back taxes because sanity prevailed in 1980 by the razor-thin margin of 5-4.

Fast-forwarding to the passage of Barack Obama's signature health-care legislation, Reilly could hardly contain himself when I brought up the subject:

> How come we're not screaming at the override? Obama
> has just destroyed the Hyde Amendment! I feel like telling
> the congressmen, "he made fools of you fellows, but you
> don't seem to care! He has all these insurance companies
> paying for abortions – it's against the law! But he doesn't
> follow the law." As for the Republicans – I'm sorry –
> they're useless! They go to Washington and they
> become spineless. Did you lose your voice? Did
> you lose your backbone? All because of deal-making
> subversion: "Do you need a new park? Do you
> need something else?" People are bought, sold, and
> delivered. And what have we got? Nothing.

When I asked Monsignor to explain how the same country that approved the Hyde Amendment could wind up disapproving it, he told me: "Hyde happened back in 1976 when many Americans were justly outraged at *Roe v. Wade*. It's hard to maintain a feeling of indignation for any length of time on an issue of right and wrong."

MAN OF ALL WORK

From the beginning, Reilly was involved in every aspect of the pro-life movement. In 1974, one year after *Roe v. Wade*, he joined

Dr. Ada Ryan, Nellie Gray, John Mawn, and others to organize the first March for Life in Washington, D.C. Fifteen thousand pro-lifers, including four busloads dispatched by Reilly from the New York City/Long Island area, circled the Capitol building and heard speeches by Dr. Ryan, founder of Nurses and Doctors for Life, and Senator James Buckley, William F. Buckley, Jr.'s brother.

Four years later, Reilly served as mouthpiece for the first of the nation's major "rescue" operations. The date was June 6, 1978, eight years before Randall Terry founded Operation Rescue. Six pro-lifers, including Reilly, entered New York's Center for Reproductive and Sexual Health, the largest free-standing facility of its kind (built by Bernard Nathanson), and their plan was simple. They would get arrested, have their day in court, and defend themselves on the basis of the common law doctrine of "necessity," which allows a person to break a law in order to achieve a higher good. One may trespass, for example, to save a child in a burning building.

Since Reilly served as media liaison for the event, he was de-lighted when *The Daily News* gave it an entire centerpiece. However, the case was never allowed to come to trial. Elsewhere, in places like St. Louis that were blessed with a more conservative ethos, judges accepted the "necessity" defense and rescuers were acquitted (until they lost in an appeals court in 1983). But not in New York. There was only one piece of good news. Nathanson was so deeply moved by the calmness and courage of Reilly and his fellow pro-lifers, both then and later, that he experienced a change of heart.[1] From being an ardent supporter of abortion, he would become militantly pro-life and eventually Catholic.

The year that Monsignor took part in the above-mentioned sit-in (1978), he also participated in a hundred-mile walk-for-life through California's Death Valley, one of the hottest places on earth. A hundred miles is equivalent to six million inches, and six million was the approximate number of children killed since *Roe v. Wade*. Participants were equipped with snake-bite kits, as well as stones to hold off coyotes.

The purpose of the walk was to highlight the need for sacrifice, along with prayer, and there was plenty of the former. After covering seventy-two miles in two days and four hours, Reilly emerged with bloodied feet and blackened toenails. "There must be an easier way," suggested one of his friends. "Yes," he replied, "we should have a hit list of the lawmakers we want taken out." The *New York Times*, latching on to the term "hit list," took it to mean a list of targets for assassination. It was another error on the part of the media, but one that did more good than harm in this case because it prompted Reilly and company to publish an actual list of the legislators they wanted to defeat in the upcoming election, and, as it turned out, eight out of ten on their "hit list" were losers!

To round out our story, Randall Terry founded Operation Rescue in 1986, and the following year, his volunteers blocked clinic entrances at Cherry Hill Women's Center on the outskirts of Philadelphia. Hundreds were arrested, and although the Center didn't close, something better happened. Fr. James Lisante of the Rockville Centre Diocese on Long Island lauded the rescuers, and on December 28, the Feast of the Holy Innocents, he brought out two bishops, 150-200 priests, and thousands of laity to picket a local abortion clinic.

Reilly himself, who, by now, was "Monsignor Reilly" and the principal at Cathedral, participated in twenty-one rescues in four states. Arrested six times but never held overnight or forced to put up bail, he gained valuable experience, and by the time he finished, he had a wide range of contacts. Dr. Mildred Jefferson, the first president of National Right to Life and first woman to graduate from Harvard Medical School (summa cum laude), was a friend, as was Joan Andrews. He and Joan were actually arrested together, and after being booked, their fingerprints went to Washington on the same form.

THE BOARD OF EDUCATION

To wind up on the wrong side of the law, as he often did in rescue situations, called for a good set of psychological shock absorbers, and it's a blessing that Monsignor had them because, for many years, he suffered one reverse after another.

Take, for example, the day he went before the New York City Board of Education and pledged the support of Catholic principals for public school teachers who were opposed to sex education in the classroom. His statement referenced studies indicating that sex education of the kind taught in most schools heightens interest in sex – the more sex ed, the more promiscuity, and the more promiscuity, the more abortion because prophylactics have a wide margin of error.

After presenting his findings, he told Board members that he planned to release them at a news conference the following day. Little did he know that his fellow principals had drawn up a paper of their own that was greatly watered down. When he heard the news at the end of the Board meeting, he was deeply saddened because this was far more than a personal setback. Catholic support would not be forthcoming, then or ever, for public school principals who wished to fight sex ed.

God, who writes straight with crooked lines, had additional disappointments in store for Monsignor Reilly, but every one of them, without exception, would work to his advantage by preparing him for a role he could never have imagined.

CHAPTER 3

THE FOUNDER

On the basis of what we have seen thus far, one might suppose that when Monsignor Reilly founded the Helpers in 1989 he was reacting to *Roe v. Wade.* He was indeed. Yet there is more to the story. I wouldn't want to minimize the importance of what happened in 1973. Yet, for the historical backdrop to be complete and the founder's motivation to be laid bare, we need to recall a series of events that struck fear into the heart of every American beginning in 1976 when Joseph Stockett firebombed a Planned Parenthood facility in Eugene, Oregon.[1]

The following year, pro-lifers set fire to a facility in St. Paul, Minnesota, and seven years later, on Christmas Eve, 1984, they firebombed three abortion mills in Pensacola, Florida, forcing two of them to close.[2] The violence soon spread to facilities in Maryland, Virginia, and Washington, D.C. In all, there were approximately 700 acts of violence against abortionists during a twenty-year period beginning in 1976, and about two hundred clinics were damaged.[3]

Fast forwarding to 1988, the year before Monsignor founded the Helpers, over a thousand of Randall Terry's operatives were arrested for trying to close down abortion mills in Atlanta, Georgia, during the Democratic National Convention. This was the year the police turned brutal (in Atlanta), and twelve hundred of Terry's demonstrators were jailed in New York City, among them Fr. Benedict Groeschel and Bishop Austin Vaughan, the brilliant rector emeritus of St. Joseph's Seminary.

America was locked in angry confrontation, and public opinion was beginning to harden, even against sit-in-type civil disobedience. Jail terms, which had averaged only a few hours during the late 1970s and early 1980s, were stretching into weeks, months, even years. Monsignor could see that violence was not the answer. In his words, "the devil was winning," and the future lay in "converting one heart at a time":

> Taking the law into your own hands . . . that's a revolt . . . . .
> Blocking the entrances to abortion clinics only delays
> the killing of babies, it doesn't stop it . . . . You have
> to convert the heart, something only God can do, and
> this requires prayer and fasting. More important than
> saving babies [the aim of civil disobedience] is saving
> the soul of the parent or that of the abortionist, and
> this requires spiritual conversion, something entirely
> different from the mere saving of physical life.[4]

Which is why he founded the Helpers of God's Precious Infants on October 7, 1989, an organization distinguished for its prayerful, non-confrontational style of witness.

Ask him how he decided on the name "Helpers of God's Precious Infants," and he will tell you that it came to him as he knelt before the Blessed Sacrament. He had planned to call his followers "Helpers of the Holy Innocents," but the Lord told him in prayer that He wanted His name in the title. He also thought that the word "holy" might be puzzling to Catholics unfamiliar with the Feast of the Holy Innocents. Hence the change to "precious." And later, when asked why he chose "precious," he answered: "Because they [the infants] belong to God and are loved by God."

The date of the founding is significant because the Helpers entrust all their work to the intercession of Mary, whose image they carry on all of their prayer vigils, and October 7 happens to be the Feast of Our Lady of the Rosary, formerly known as the feast of Our Lady of Victory after the defeat of the Turkish fleet in the Battle of Lepanto.

One of Monsignor's favorite stories illustrating the benefit of invoking the help of the Blessed Mother harks back to the time when he was crossing from Hungary into Croatia on his way to give a three-day course on Helpers methods to priests in Medjugorje. He found the border closed, with trucks lined up as far back as the eye could see. Burly Croat farmers were protesting the importation of Hungarian produce that undercut native sales. Reilly ordered his driver to bypass the trucks, and when he reached the checkpoint and was told he could not pass, he said to one of the guards, "Mary wants me to get through so I can speak to her priests." The giant of a man listened, then replied that he would have to consult his supervisor. On returning, he asked incredulously, "Mary wants you to go through?" "Yes," Monsignor replied. "Mary wants me to go through." And so it was. He went through. Call it moxie, call it chutzpah. For the man from Maspeth it was "the woman" of Genesis.

THE EARLY YEARS

It only took the Helpers six months to grow in number from six to thirty under the mantle of Mary's protection. Seminarians from Cathedral Prep swelled their ranks, and by 1993, Monsignor had counselors at seventeen out of forty clinics in the New York/New Jersey area.

On hindsight, we know that he had a winning formula capable of working wonders. But his Helpers experienced the usual ups and downs of any fledgling organization. City permits didn't always specify enough space between police barricades to allow them to gather as a group. The distance required by the police between counselors and clinic entrances could be problematical too, and on top of all this, Monsignor had to deal with complaints from shop owners who objected to his hymn singing. When they begged him to hold his vigils earlier in the day so patrons wouldn't be discouraged from coming, he agreed. But this allowed clinic owners to schedule appointments at times when his people were no longer present. One clinic owner, furious at the Helpers, grew his business by advertising abortion, while another built a second clinic.

A UNIQUE POLICE-PROTECTED VIGIL FORMAT

In case readers are unfamiliar with the format of a typical prayer vigil, it is police-protected and begins with the celebration of the Eucharist at a neighborhood church. When Mass ends, walkie-talkie amplifiers are distributed, along with song sheets, and after exposition of the Blessed Sacrament, the priest or layman in charge of the vigil begins recitation of the Rosary from a kneeling position at the foot of the altar. Then, while still on the first decade, he leads the congregation out of the church. Those unable to join the march remain behind in prayer.

Familiar hymns such as "Hail Holy Queen" are sung after each decade. It's the Joyful Mysteries on the way to the clinic, followed, on site, by the Sorrowful and Glorious. Before returning to church, Monsignor asks everyone to "kneel humbly for one minute of prayer in absolute silence" imploring God to forgive all who are involved in the killing, and on the way home, he leads the Luminous Mysteries. Last of all comes Benediction, a practice which underscores the Real Presence of Jesus in the Eucharist and, as such, is a boon during the current age of skepticism. It had fallen into such disuse after Vatican II that Reilly was hard put, on occasion, to find a monstrance in the host church!

NO TALKING PLEASE

Another practice cherished by the Helpers is that of reverential silence. Monsignor views it as so vital to the success of a prayer vigil that he urges counselors to assemble a block away from the clinic entrance and disassemble at the same distance. He knows, of course, that people like to talk. But years of experience have taught him that passersby need to see people praying, rather than chatting, if they are to sense that they are in the presence of an abomination.

KEY PERSONALITIES

Much of the credit for the founding of the Helpers goes to its charter members: Frances Moore (Monsignor's sister) and Frances' daughter, Eileen, along with three grandparents who were introduced earlier as parishioners of St. Teresa's : John Collins, his wife Adelaide, and Rosemary Abruzzino. For over a decade, Frances served as the Helpers' treasurer, maintaining a supply room in Queens and shipping informational packets, as well as videos, to anyone interested in starting a Helpers chapter.

The pro bono legal work of Kathleen O'Connell will be the subject of a separate chapter. But it should be said, by way of preface, that she not only defeated a multi-million-dollar law suit and intervened repeatedly to prevent the police from interfering with the work of Monsignor's street counselors; she also thwarted efforts on the part of both New York City and Jersey City to obtain paralyzing injunctions. Three times she blocked the New York City Council when it sought to strip the Helpers of their First Amendment rights.

On the spiritual side, Fr. Benedict Groeschel, CFR, co-founder of the Franciscan Friars of the Renewal, led many of Monsignor's prayer vigils, including the first ever held in Manhattan. Once it became clear that Operation Rescue was on the ropes, he and Reilly were among the first to see the need for an alternate means of invigorating the pro-life movement. The friars helped with the foundation of Helpers branches in Great Britain, and many years later, when Groeschel hosted EWTN's popular "Sunday Night Prime," he had Monsignor on the show as a special guest.

We come finally to the person of Thomas Daily, Supreme Chaplain of the Knights of Columbus, whose no-nonsense style of leadership surfaced the moment he was named bishop of Brooklyn (February, 1990). In response to a reporter's question, he let it be known that New York's governor, Mario Cuomo, would not be welcome to speak at his parishes because, as he put it, Cuomo had "a problem. . . . A Catholic politician should have consistency, especially on this issue [of abortion]." Asked whether he agreed with Bishop Vaughan that Cuomo was risking damnation, Daily hesitated, then replied, "Yes, I do."[4]

It was all of a piece. When the owner of Brooklyn's largest abortion facility offered to forego abortions one day a week if the Helpers ceased praying, Daily told him that as long as there was killing, the vigils would continue. His stand on homosexuality was equally forthright. Voicing support for Courage, a group that encourages gays to remain chaste, he described homosexuality as an orientation that must be controlled.

There were bishops who put pro-life activism on a par with campaigns to reduce poverty, homelessness, and capital punishment based on the "seamless garment" theory. But Daily disagreed vehemently, rejecting out of hand any comparison between quality of life issues and the right of a child to be born.[5]

He was anxious for one of his priests to found a religious order dedicated to the pro-life cause, and since no one was better suited for the job than Reilly, he offered him the position, along with some property. Monsignor felt honored by Daily's offer, but he knew from years of experience as a school principal what such a post would entail. It would keep him from doing what he did best, which was counseling at abortion mills and training others to do the same. As head of a religious order, he would have to pour the lion's share of his time into academic planning, faculty supervision, campus mainte-nance, and fund raising. Then, too, if he wanted to send his priests and sisters overseas, he would have to teach them languages. He much preferred drawing upon the talents of native speakers.

The other motive behind Reilly's refusal was his belief in the power of ordinary men and women to serve as prayer warriors and street counselors. Hadn't Vatican II called for greater lay involve-ment in the Church's mission? And wasn't the Holy Father urging Catholics to take to the streets as part of "the new evangelization"? This is precisely what he envisaged!

On the one hand, he knew that the involvement of priests and bishops was essential, for without the grace of the Sacraments, the laity could not do battle with the culture of death.[6] On the other, he believed that simple men and women from every walk of life make the best shock troops, and invoking Scripture, he recalled that Our Lord, after teaching His apostles how to fish for souls, had left them to their own devices.

Daily's greatest contribution to the founding of the Helpers was his willingness to lead monthly prayer vigils. His constant presence at Monsignor's side was not only a striking episcopal endorsement of the Helpers' approach to pro-life witness. It brought the faith-ful out in force and generated much-needed publicity. If Daily led 700 people in prayer for an hour in pouring rain, as happened at

Interfaith Medical Center on one occasion, all who read *The Tablet* would know about it.

Daily was a man who knew the meaning of the word "perseverance." After praying before a particular abortion mill for forty-two consecutive days, he had the satisfaction of seeing it close. Following retirement, he could be found, Saturday after Saturday, at the entrance to a Forest Hills clinic, rosary in hand. Why? Because abortion, in his view, was "the primordial evil of our society," and it struck him as puzzling "that more and more of our clergy, religious, and laity do not take up the Rosary and exercise a bit of penance to walk to an abortion place and simply pray, knowing in faith that one Hail Mary can change the world."[7]

During the early 1990s, when he led anywhere from 400 to 1,000 Helpers on a given Saturday, dozens of counter-demonstrators would come out, and scores of police officers were needed to keep order. One heard cat calls, along with song parodies designed to drown out the Helpers' prayer. On one occasion, five male protesters appeared dressed as women. Daily simply kept his head bowed in prayer.

More recently, I've heard pro-choice protesters blow trumpets and beat drums during a prayer vigil. I've seen clinic workers dance to rock and roll while shouting, "Keep your rosaries off our ovaries!" Many is the time I've felt the challenge of the world. But one thing is certain. Conditions today are civil by comparison with what Reilly and company faced during the early years of their campaign.

WHAT HAPPENED AT CHOICES

On June 11, 1990, Choices Women's Medical Center on Queens Boulevard in Rego Park, N.Y. became the target of the first Helpers' prayer vigil led by a bishop. It was the largest abortion mill in the city, the site of 10% of all New York State abortions -- about 20,000 annually. Monsignor saw to it that every Catholic in the diocese knew that the vigil would be led by Bishop Daily, and in his preliminary letter to pastors, he provided inserts for Sunday bulletins calling attention to the enormity of abortion's death toll and asking parishioners how they would feel if every first and second grader at every Catholic school in the city were to be murdered because this was how many unborn children were slaughtered every year in the wombs of New York mothers.

The response was overwhelming. A hundred NYPD officers ensured the safety of a thousand marchers, and Daily was flanked by such luminaries as Bishop Vaughan and Fr. Groeschel. During the bilingual recitation of the Rosary, pro-choicers blew whistles to drown out the bishop's prayers. Lewd chants echoed through the air. Gays held up signs reading "HOMOPHOBES!" Nothing out of the ordinary.

Police captains, aware of Monsignor's record of arrests for civil disobedience, parked an extra busload of riot-control officers around the corner just in case. "I was reformed," Reilly says with a chuckle, "but they didn't believe me! I was tired of being carried away by the police. So I brought them with me! Which is what I've been doing ever since. This way, when the abortion clinic calls for help, as they generally do, the men in blue are on my side. When they arrive, the first thing they do is come to me for briefing!"

Following the vigil, a second Helpers letter went out to pastors thanking them for their support and setting the record straight regarding the effect of the Helpers' presence:

> The mill's owner said there were no cancellations, but he didn't mention that at least 80% [of his customers] were no-shows. Away from the site, only God knows how many distressed women chose life as they watched on TV or saw pictures in the newspapers the next day of the Bishop leading God's people in prayers and hymns . . . . Millions of people once again became acutely aware of the slaughter in our midst of the innocent unborn. God has blessed us abundantly.

What Monsignor didn't say because he didn't know it at the time was that this was the beginning of the end for eighteen out of forty-two abortion providers in the Brooklyn diocese. No demonstration of Catholic determination to end abortion could have been more impressive than what occurred that day, and it wasn't long before other bishops in other cities began following Daily's example.

PRECIOUS BLOOD

In June of 1991, something happened that would have a tremendous impact on the future of the Helpers. Monsignor relocated. Moving from Cathedral Prep to the Monastery of the Precious

Blood in Sunset Park, Brooklyn, he was not far from the Verrazano Bridge. When I asked him why, he was candid. While running a pro-life club at Cathedral Prep, he had led students on anti-abortion prayer vigils, and anything remotely connected with pro-life protest in those days was viewed as dangerously provocative.

No doubt, other factors were at work as well. Admissions officers may have feared that the kind of student activities he was sponsoring would hurt recruitment because the man who succeeded Reilly as principal told him flat-out that priests in the diocese were reluctant to send students to Cathedral on account of his pro-life emphasis. His championship of the rights of the unborn and all the traveling this entailed must have taken its toll. Then, too, his record of arrests for civil disobedience raised the specter of litigation.

Whatever the reason, Reilly resigned as principal of Cathedral Prep two years after founding the Helpers, and no sooner had he done so than his successor told him to his face: "It would be best if you removed yourself totally from the building by not even living here any longer" (to the best of Reilly's recollection). It had come to this. He had no promise of future employment, and his students were affected as well.

Before Reilly left Cathedral, morale had been high. A certain number of seniors entered the seminary each year after graduation. But soon after his departure, vocations dried up. Although the vocations crisis can be seen as part of a trend beginning in the 1960s and 1970s, there is another side to the coin: young people want to give their all to a noble cause, and the teachers they admire most are the ones who have their eyes on the stars, as well as their feet on the ground.

What's interesting about Monsignor's case is how closely it resembles what happened to Fr. Marx prior to his founding of Human Life International. Marx had nowhere to lay his head after being ejected by an academic institution, and like Reilly, he was redirected by the Almighty to full-time work for the pro-life cause.

In Reilly's case, it didn't take long for the hidden hand of the Lord to show itself. At the very moment he found himself jobless, the chaplain of the Monastery of the Precious Blood died and Bishop Daily needed a replacement.

The Monastery may have been out of the loop geographically, but it was a blessing because it afforded the Helpers much needed room to expand. In comparison with the single room they occupied at Cathedral, they now had spacious quarters consisting of an office, a residential suite, a handsome conference room, and, for visitors, a dozen guest rooms. If there was any doubt as to the providential nature of Monsignor's transfer to Precious Blood, it vanished when John Paul II published an encyclical letter in 1995 identifying the source for the victory of the pro-life movement as the "Precious Blood of Our Lord."[8]

CHAPTER 4

THE VICTOR

I f Bishop Daily's decision to throw the full weight of his office behind the Helpers was the first big step forward for Monsignor, a second was not long in coming. Cardinal Mahony, head of the bishops' Right to Life Committee in 1992, sent a newsletter to all dioceses endorsing the Helpers. At the same time, he led 1100 Helpers through the streets of Los Angeles. It was not the first prayer vigil the city had ever seen or even the first led by a bishop, but it was the first with a cardinal out front, and it paved the way for similar action by other princes of the Church.

There was the usual opposition. Planned Parenthood came out in force, as did members of the American Civil Liberties Union and some Protestant ministers. Fortunately, units of the California Highway Patrol and officers on horseback were on hand as well. [1]

Following the example of Daily and Mahony, six other cardinals, along with over a hundred bishops were soon leading Helpers vigils. Twelve hundred prayer warriors followed Cardinal George in Chicago. Cardinal Rigali's vigil of two thousand became a lead story for the influential St. Louis *Post-Dispatch*. Meanwhile, in

Monsignor's home town, Cardinal O'Connor marched at the head of a crowd numbering upwards of twenty-five hundred.

The O'Connor march, which was momentous, not only for the Helpers, but also for the pro-life movement in general, will be given its due in chapter 5. But first, we must address an important question, that of effectiveness. How effective have the Helpers been when it comes to saving babies' lives?

"OFFICE SPACE AVAILABLE"

The short answer to the question is: "very effective." Their mere presence is enough to cause businesses sharing a building with an abortionist to pull out. "Office Space Available" signs appear in the windows of a bank or Radio Shack. Subsequently, property owners refuse to renew the abortionist's lease. Mill owners have to move, and such moves are never advantageous. Take Choices, for example, the target of Bishop Daily's 1991 prayer vigil. Each time it relocated under Helpers pressure, its abortion count dropped – from 20,000 annually before its first move, to 15,000 before the second move, to 10,000 thereafter.

A second measure of success for the Helpers is the number of turnarounds. They reported 113 in the Brooklyn diocese during their first three months – a little over ten per week or about one per week at each of the sites. But as they grew more comfortable with their work and acquired the necessary skills, the number of "saves" increased. Taking Choices as an example once again, ninety or more clients would show up on a given Saturday between 7 and

11:30 AM. But after twenty-six weeks of prayer and counseling, the number was down to thirty-one with forty turnarounds.

There was the time when thirty-eight out of seventy-five women who entered a mill after receiving counseling came back out with their babies. At two o'clock in the afternoon on that particular day, the mill's anesthesiologist, a man complicit in thousands of abortions, walked up to Monsignor, and said, "May I speak to you?" "Surely," Monsignor replied. "From now on, I'm having nothing more to do with abortion," he announced, "I will limit myself to healing."[2] His words were not without effect. It wasn't long before other staff members, sharing a similar sentiment, were moved to seek alternate work.

By 1991, the number of turnarounds or "saves" in metropolitan New York had increased to 600 on a yearly basis.[3] Forty-four were reported in the Brooklyn diocese on a single Saturday.[4] The Helpers were on a roll, and they had friends. One lady presented them with a cake she'd baked as a special token of appreciation.[5] A rabbi stopped by to give moral support.

How did they do it? By being extremely patient and extremely helpful. A couple with four children on their way to a mill to terminate their fifth pregnancy were offered financial aid, assistance in finding a seven-room apartment, and a job for the husband. This was all they needed.[6]

Every time Monsignor leads a prayer vigil, there are women inside the mill who get so tense at the sound of pro-life prayer and singing that the doctor can't do a pelvic exam. Some of them go home, never to return. Others, on arrival at the mill, are so struck by the presence of prayer warriors that they never climb out of their car, while still others turn away on foot.

HIDDEN FACTORS

Not all results are measurable. If, for instance, the Helpers see a woman leaving an abortion mill, they can usually tell from the expression on her face whether or not she has saved her baby.[7] On the other hand, she may enter a mill late in the day and take two hours to change her mind. If so, Reilly's people will never know because they are no longer on site.

Cancellations are a second hidden factor. We have it from one of Australia's leading child killers that for every twenty women who book an abortion, one or two will be no-shows when the Helpers are present, and, by comparison with results elsewhere, this is small change. One Saturday in August of 1990 at TLC Clinic in Long Island City, not a single abortion took place. The only woman who entered the building during the Helpers' vigil came right out. At another clinic, one of the doctors was a no-show. So many customers failed to keep their appointments at a third facility one Saturday (the busiest day of the week for abortionists) that the clinic ceased doing business on Saturday.

THE BIG PICTURE

By 1998, only nine years into the life of the Helpers, over thirty abortuaries had closed in the state of New York, and in

Rockland County, where Monsignor's prayer warriors were specially active, the number of mills dropped from six to zero. The nation as a whole showed a 17.4 percent drop in abortion, accompanied by a rapid decrease in the number of clinics around the country -- from 2,000 to 720 in the decade after 1993.[8] A Congressional ban on partial birth abortion was upheld by the Supreme Court in 2006, and the annual March for Life, which began with fifteen thousand in 1974, was soon attracting hundreds of thousands, most of them under the age of thirty, with burgeoning numbers of youth attending Students for Life conferences as a prelude to the March.

Fewer and fewer medical facilities were willing to perform abortions.[9] Half of all the nation's abortions in 1973 were done by hospitals, but by 1992, the figure was down to 7%.[10] Residency training programs fell off, and recruitment of doctors and other staff personal became increasingly difficult.[11] Finally, as abortionists lost the respect of their fellow doctors, more and more were denied hospital privileges. In time, the shortage of doctors willing to kill became so acute that abortion providers began turning to physicians' assistants, nurse-practitioners, and mid-wives.[12]

Most impressive of all, a majority of Americans began describing themselves as "pro-life," with young adults aged 29 and under especially staunch in their commitment to life and chastity. In 1992, 26% of Americans were strongly pro-life, with 43% pro-choice; but by 2006, the percentages had been reversed with 41% strongly pro-life and only 30% pro-choice.

PROGRESS OVERSEAS

Slowly but surely, Monsignor's method of prayerful, peaceful protest spread from Brooklyn to other parts of the world. The papal nuncio to the United Nations led a Helpers vigil; the Vatican's Pontifical Council on the Family informed bishops overseas of the Helpers apostolate; and by 2005, the message had reached almost every country in Europe, including Poland and Hungary.

As of this writing, Reilly has visited Australia five times, spoken in the principal urban centers of New Zealand, and borne witness to the sacredness of human life in places as far removed as Riga (Latvia) and Cape Town (South Africa). The Helpers are in Ukraine, Moldova, South Korea, Portugal, Nigeria, India, Sri Lanka, Belarus and Albania (where Monsignor appeared on a nation-wide "60 Minutes-type" TV program) – approximately thirty countries altogether, on six continents.

There is no better indication of the kind of geographical reach attained by the Helpers in their early years than two of Monsignor's overseas itineraries from the turn of the century. Itinerary #1: Germany (Frankfurt, Munster, Stuttgart), Austria (Bregenz), Switzerland (St. Galen), Germany (Fulda, Augsburg, and Munich where a Helpers vigil was shown on German TV), Slovakia (Bratislava), Hungary (where Monsignor delivered an address in Budapest on prime-time TV), Croatia (Zagreb), Bosnia (Medjugorje), Rome, and London. Itinerary #2: England, Ireland, Spain, France (including Paris, Lourdes, Toulouse, and Thiel sur Acolin), Belgium, Holland, Germany (Nuremburg, Munich, Kaufbeuren, Germaringen, and

Obergermaringen), Switzerland, Hungary, Slovakia, Austria (Vienna and Graz), and then back to Bosnia (Medjugorje) before returning to New York.

If we take into account domestic travel, which was every bit as extensive as travel abroad, Monsignor logged an average of 26,000 miles per year. Sixty cities in thirty-seven states of the Union have Helpers chapters, and Reilly has visited all of them.

For the record, not all anti-abortion vigils are led by Helpers. Most, however, are either Helpers inspired or Helpers formatted. One example would be an overseas organization called "With Christ for Life" which is not run by Helpers, but which utilizes the Reilly method to save babies at scores of sites in Italy. Here at home, there are five groups that use Monsignor's methods for every actual Helpers chapter.

SACRIFICE

The success enjoyed by the Helpers, as well as by the anti-abortion movement in general, is striking, particularly in light of all the futile efforts that have been made to check other forms of immorality such as fornication, contraception, euthanasia, and sodomy. Abortion is murder, and, as such, it makes a good target. But another reason for Reilly's success comes down to a single word: sacrifice. There has been more "skin off the back," so to speak, in the battle for the unborn than in all the other moral battles combined, and the Helpers have sacrificed as much as anyone. Mother Angelica of EWTN fame once observed that "if you want to accomplish the miraculous, you

better be prepared to do the ridiculous." If there is any better description of what Monsignor's people do than this, I have yet to hear of it.
St. Paul would call them "fools for Christ" (1 Cor. 4:10).

One reads in the Letter to the Hebrews that there is no remission
of sin without the shedding of blood.[13] The Helpers may not have
bled as the martyrs did, but direct, hands-on confrontation with
evil can be daunting. Typical is what happened on a cold winter
morning when Monsignor and Bishop Daily arrived at a church in
Brooklyn Heights to prepare for a prayer vigil. The locks on three
of the front doors, as well as one on the side, were jammed with glue
and knife blades. All four had to be replaced. Fortunately, the pastor
was able to enter by a back door.[14]

Lawn sprinklers have been turned on the Helpers; pro-abortion
supporters have pelted them with tomatoes; they have been spat
upon. A man dumped a pail of water on them from an apartment
three stories above the ground.[15] On another occasion, a pack of
sixteen clinic escorts, attempting to provoke an incident, pushed
Reilly to the wall. There was the time, too, when, he was hit by an
egg. One of his counselors came up to him and said, "Monsignor,
this is terrible; what are we going to do?" And he replied: "Take a
picture!"[16]

Rotten eggs have not stopped the Helpers, and neither have
death threats. Police arrived one Saturday morning at St. Michael's
Church in Sunset Park with a bomb-sniffing dog. After searching
every one of church's nooks and crannies, no explosives were found;
but during that day's vigil, a man dressed as a woman sang a blas-
phemous song, while a real woman accompanied him on the tuba.[17]

I like to think that Monsignor, taking it all in stride, would agree with G. K. Chesterton, who remarked that he liked "getting into hot water . . . [because it] keeps you clean."

THE H BOMB

One doesn't normally think of prayer as a form of sacrifice, but to be fruitful, it requires effort, and, at its fruitful best, it is the most powerful weapon in Monsignor's arsenal. Right from the start, he could see that if the nation's moral free fall was ever to be arrested, Americans would have to undergo a change of heart. He knew, too, that such a change lies solely within God's province, and so he used prayer to invoke the intercessory power of the Lord and His Blessed Mother. This is why the Helpers, in their early years, conducted prayer vigils at all of New York's abortuaries from noon on Good Friday to noon the following day. It likewise explains why they flocked to Wednesday evening hours of Eucharistic adoration at his monastery, as well as at Mary Help of Christians parish in Woodside, Queens.

Prayer was their H Bomb, and it still is. The faithful souls who make the Helpers' rosaries, including an arthritic woman of 85, are asked to pray over each set of beads for the person to whom it goes. Monsignor will ask every woman who seems beyond reclamation as she approaches an abortion clinic, "May I give you the gift of a rosary?" and the effect, in his words, is unbelievable: "I cannot tell you how many times they'll go to the door of the clinic, rosary in hand. Then it begins. They turn back."

The number of turnarounds at an abortion mill is directly proportional to the number of persons on the ground praying.[18] And again, Monsignor has a story. One day, his counselors suggested that he speak to a man smoking a cigarette. The man's girlfriend had gone into the mill to do away with their baby, but he himself seemed ambivalent. So Monsignor walked up to him and said, "Young man, you'd better put that cigarette out." "Why?" he asked. "Because you are going into the clinic to bring your girlfriend out." After a few minutes of counseling, the man softened, and Reilly fired off an SOS to his people: "We are in need of some serious help for that couple. Please pray the Divine Mercy Chaplet." Falling to their knees, they got to work and were on the second decade when Monsignor felt a tap on his shoulder. It was the young man. "I thought I told you to go inside and bring her out," Monsignor said to him. "I did," stammered the man, pointing to the woman standing behind him. He had talked her out of having an abortion, and she was crying.

Monsignor began sharing his joy with the young woman and her boyfriend when another couple came along who had been converted by the first couple; and while he was congratulating them, a third couple came up. After talking with couple #2, they, too, had opted out of abortion! By this time, he had more on his plate than he could handle, and so he told his prayer warriors, still on their knees storming heaven: "Slow down; I can't handle this!"

Examples of the power of prayer could fill volumes. Every day for six years, a group of Hispanic men and women came to pray with Monsignor. As he tells it, "One of the men at the age of seventy-five held his arms high for forty-five minutes! Try doing this some time. You'll find it's not easy. The group maintained perfect silence and some knelt through fifteen decades. One man, aged 84, would run down to the abortion clinic and spend six hours every day. It's amazing. We never had a day there with the group present when there wasn't at least one turnaround."

Because of the importance Monsignor attaches to prayer, he always recruits as many "pray-ers" as he can before taking to the street. To assemble what he called his "power pack" in 1989, he went to schools and asked students if they would be willing to pray for his Helpers, adopt them by name, and make a special sacrifice such as giving up a night of television. When he visited sisters confined to infirmaries and nursing homes, he would ask them to offer up their suffering in line with Paul's Letter to the Colossians: "What is lacking in the sufferings of Christ, I fill up in my flesh."[19] The more pain they reported, the better he liked it – to the point of joking: "Do you suffer a lot, Sister?" "Yes," she replied. "Marvelous!" said Monsignor, "more graces!"

It was a "dream," he says, when twenty-six Felician sisters promised to pray for his counselors by name. The Carmelites in Dachau, Germany, followed suit, as did the sisters at Pius XII Monastery at Fatima, along with the Sisters of St. Joseph in Brentwood, New York. Hundreds of Dominicans at an Amityville infirmary entered the lists. For the Sisters Adorers of the Precious Blood, who do Monsignor's laundry, cook his meals, clean his rooms, and sing like angels at his Masses, prayer is what they do. "You don't know who they are," Reilly tells his Helpers, "but they spend their life praying for you and praising God. I have one sister who has been in a bed of pain approximately thirty years – pain every day – and when I come back from a six-hour stand outside the mills, she'll say, 'Well, how did you do?' I tell her it is not what WE do, but rather what YOU do that counts. Prayer is all-powerful."

MORTIFICATION

Next to prayer in terms of purchase power is fasting.[20] But Monsignor makes a point of telling his Helpers that they don't have to fast from food:

> If such fasting makes you think about food night and day, let it go. What's your favorite TV program? Skip it once in a while. Do you like to smoke? Go without it for a spell. And be careful not to take pride in your fasting. Don't be like the Pharisees who thought of themselves as better than other men: 'I fast twice a week, I give tithes . . . . .' Fasting is a means to an end, not an end in itself. And it is required because we are up against Satan, who calls good evil and evil good.

Since Reilly never asks a Helper to do more than he himself has done, one is not surprised to learn that he skips lunch and doesn't take his breakfast until after he's finished counseling. I was told that he eats whatever is put before him for dinner, with one exception -- for years, the Sisters couldn't get him to take cookies or other sweets. He has a prized parakeet named "BJ," whose cage sits atop a table in his living room and whose chirps are apt to elicit an affectionate response. One day after morning Mass, I asked him if BJ had been fed. "No," he told me, "BJ will not eat until I do." Imagine a bird this sympatico. It's awesome! And you want to know something? Fasting hasn't done BJ any harm. He's reached a ripe old age and his master absolutely dotes on him!

THE ELEMENT OF FORGIVENESS

When the forces of evil come up against prayer, mortification, and risk-taking, they have met their match. But our success story would be incomplete without a word about a fourth and final component of Reilly's winning combination: namely, the emphasis placed upon forgiveness. As he puts it:

When a woman who has had an abortion asks us the question, "Could God ever truly love me again?" our response is short and simple. "Mom, God never stopped loving you." It is we who turn away from God, become enemies of God, but God never became an enemy of us. When the whole world was broken and estranged . . . . . God, in his unconditional, merciful love, came into the human condition and freely offered his life in our place in reparation for our sins . . . . . Those involved in abortion are putting their eternal salvation at risk. But they have every reason to be joyful after repentance because even though a great physical evil has been done to the unborn, innocent child, that same child goes straight to heaven because it is impossible to sin before the age of reason.

Following an abortion, all of the people involved, but
especially the mothers, experience low self-esteem,
depression, and despair. Some are so blinded by the
culture of death that they just don't appreciate the
wrongness of what they are doing until after the abortion
has taken place. It is then, especially, that they need to
experience the unconditional, merciful love of God.

NATHANSON'S GOAL

It is interesting to note, in this connection, that Dr. Nathanson
wanted what he called "the gold standard" of mercy. When he found
it in the Church of Rome, he converted, and when I say "the Church
of Rome," I'm thinking, in particular, of the Helpers who pray not
only for the repentance of parents, but also for God's mercy on the
unrepentant, including the abortionist. "It is not us versus them
[with] the enemy on one side and the good guys on the other,"
says Monsignor, "you can't think of anyone as your enemy. Christ
Himself never regarded anyone as an 'enemy.'"[21] Another way of
putting it, again in Reilly's words, is that "being on the side of the
unborn doesn't give us the right to be uncharitable towards the sin-
ner." As for the babies, they come last in the order of prayer because
their place in heaven is assured.

STANDING AT CALVARY

Reilly envisions his Helpers as contemplatives standing at
Calvary, and also as channels through which Christ grants forgiveness

to those enslaved by the culture of death. They must therefore "get out of God's way" by removing from their presence anything that would prevent those inside or outside an abortion mill from experiencing the boundless love expressed by Jesus on the Cross. There is no passage in the Gospels that means more to him than ten words spoken by Our Lord in excruciating pain: "Father, forgive them, for they know not what they do":

> These words should be ours when we stand outside the abortion mill. We must be able to absorb their cursing, no matter how difficult. The kind of self-righteousness that fuels hatred must be totally eliminated. Our attitude must always be: "There, but for the grace of God, go I." We have received a gift from God bought by Christ's passion and death, rather than by anything we, as finite human beings, may ever have done. Therefore, there must not be anything in our demeanor or manner on the street to suggest confrontation, anger, or debate. If we bring light to darkness, God will do the rest.

Because he knows that fifty percent of the women who come for an abortion have already killed one or more babies, he hastens to assure them of God's forgiveness provided they are sorry. This lessens the likelihood of their having another abortion. But even if they turn a deaf ear and resort to murder once again, they will be more likely to repent when post-abortive trauma sets in because they will remember what they heard.

To prevent women who have had an abortion from losing hope after they feel the sting of remorse, Monsignor founded Rachel's

Helpers. Not to be confused with Rachel's Vineyard, which offers re-
treats for men and women who suffer from post-abortion syndrome,
the Helpers' program, launched under the direction of Florence
Maloney, Ed.D., is an eleven-week Bible study. In essence, it is a
mutual support group along the lines of Alcoholics Anonymous.
Participants meet confidentially with those who are similarly trou-
bled, and together, in a small group, they focus on Scriptural pas-
sages that highlight God's willingness to forgive any sin, however
grave. There are no fees, but lots of sympathy, along with light
refreshments.

The best of Reilly's reclamation stories features a man named
Joey, who had nothing to do with abortion, but was miraculously
converted from a hopeless life of addiction at a Protestant mission. With grace, he became a humble servant who didn't regard
any task as beneath him because he did everything with love. One
evening, at a prayer service, a repentant drunk came up to the altar
and, kneeling down, cried out to God for help. He kept shouting,
"O God, make me like Joey! Make me like Joey! Make me like
Joey!" The minister leaned over and said to the man, "Son, I think
it would be better if you prayed 'Make me like Jesus!' The man
looked up at the minister with a puzzled expression and asked, "Is
Jesus like Joey?"

THE VIRTUE OF CHARITY

Monsignor reminds his people every so often that the mainline media paints a false picture of two sides locked in mortal

combat. "Thank the Lord," he says, "we have been given this power to love those who reject us, even those who hate us. It's called the virtue of charity, and those who teach us best how to stand at our modern-day Calvary are, of course, Mary, the mother of Jesus, along with John, the beloved disciple and the holy women who stood nearby."

Although every Helper exemplifies the spirit of forgiveness, one, in particular, stands out: the late Detective Steven McDonald of the New York Police, who accompanied Monsignor on many of his prayer vigils. In 1986, while chasing a suspect in Central Park, he was shot in the face, leaving him with wounds so serious that his surgeon feared the worst. Thereafter, he was a paraplegic confined to a wheelchair and forced to breathe through a tracheal tube. But this is not what made him special in God's eyes. When his wife gave birth to a son six months after the shooting, he saw it as a wake-up call from the Lord telling him to "live, and live differently," which is what he did.

As the months passed, McDonald began to lead a life of intense prayer, asking God to better him as a person and receiving, as the fruit of his prayer, a desire to forgive the man who injured him. "I wanted to free myself," he recalled, "of all the negative, destructive emotions that his act of violence had unleashed in me . . . anger, bitterness, hatred, and other feelings. I needed to free myself of those emotions so that I could love my wife and our child and those around us . . . . I believe the only thing worse than receiving a bullet in my spine would have been to nurture revenge in my heart." His wife, Patti Ann, agrees: "In order for us to get along as a couple, I had to let go of my anger."[22]

Why dwell on the quality of mercy? Because it informs nearly all that Monsignor has to say on the subject of pro-life witness. As he tells his followers, "We're there [on the street] for the salvation of souls, to bring hope where there is despair, to bring life where there's death."

CHAPTER 5

THE TACTICIAN

We have seen what happens when someone who is spiritually energized founds an organization driven by prayer and mortification. Otherworldliness is the key to Monsignor's success. This does not mean, though, that it is the only key. Given the nature of the challenges he has faced over the years, it is doubtful that he would ever have prevailed without the gift of wiliness in temporal affairs. And so it is to the worldly side of his apostolate that we turn in this chapter, beginning with a series of vignettes.

Picture Monsignor, if you will, nearing the entrance to Brooklyn's Ambulatory Surgery Center on 43rd Street (hereafter referred to as Ambulatory). He finds clippings of priestly sex abuse on the wall in front of him, and it doesn't take him long to post a message of his own: "THE ULTIMATE CHILD ABUSER IS THE ABORTIONIST IN THIS FACILITY!" The next day, his message is gone -- and so are the clippings.

Imagine him next outside Planned Parenthood on Court Street. A piece of masonry falls from the wall. "This could be dangerous," he tells Kathy, a fellow counselor, "Better call 911." She does, and after giving her address and reporting what happened, the operator asks, "Is

anyone's life endangered?" By a stroke of Providence, her phone dies
at that moment, creating an exaggerated sense of urgency. Five fire
trucks, sirens blaring, pull up to the clinic. The abortionists, looking down from their perch above the street, are beside themselves.
Commotion of any kind is bad for business, and, rubbing salt in the
wound, Monsignor finds a way to improve on the occasion. To a fire-
man examining a piece of fallen masonry, he says, "That's dangerous.
Shut this place down!" On his return, he finds scaffolding running the
full length of the clinic sidewalk, which, for weeks to come, will not
only protect him from the elements but also oblige clients to walk right
past his counselors.

In another incident, a man comes up to the Helpers at Ambulatory
with an announcement. "The world is going to end at 2 P.M.," he
says. Sensing mischief, Reilly dismisses his associates and comes
back at the alleged time of reckoning with a photographer. Together
they stand under the Gowanus Expressway waiting for events to un-
fold. Newsmen with TV cameras arrive, followed by a busload of
radical feminists, representatives of NOW and NARAL, who have
statements they wish to read to the press. Monsignor is amused,
knowing that what they are about to say won't make any sense in
the absence of the Helpers. "Here they are again," declares one of
the feminists, "harassing the poor women who come for help in a
time of distress." Reporters and TV technicians look around. "Here
they are"? Where? The crowd knows it has been hoodwinked, and
so does the station manager at one of the TV networks whose evening report on the affair is entitled, "Much Ado About Nothing" (or
words to that effect).

The TV people are especially irked because this isn't the first time the wool has been pulled over their eyes. Their memory is still fresh of a time, once before, when the folks at Ambulatory deceived them, claiming to have photographic evidence of Helpers setting fire to their clinic. Taking the Ambulatory people at their word, the station had broadcast footage showing a hydrant behind the spot where the fire was said to have broken out. But Monsignor, after watching the falsified footage on his TV, knew at once that the hydrant being shown wasn't anywhere near the spot where the Helpers did their counseling -- it was on the opposite side of the building! Immediately, he had called the station to complain. This was defamation, pure and simple. He didn't want to sue for millions, but what was the alternative, he asked? What were they going to do to repair the damage to his reputation? Their answer was not long in coming. That very night they broadcast a retraction.

Reilly prayed and counseled at Ambulatory on 43rd Street for nineteen years in the company of such faithful associates as Maureen O'Dea, Rose Diaz, and Mike Marino. There were turnarounds, as well as cancellations; and as time passed, staff members, doctors included, began having second thoughts about abortion. Defections followed, one after another, and since this was more than the owner had bargained for, he sold his mill to a party that reopened it as a clean health facility – one that wouldn't even dispense abortifacients.[1] The oldest and largest abortion provider in the United States -- a place where a quarter of a million children had been slaughtered – was no more as of September 1, 2012.

Monsignor calls it "the Miracle on 43rd Street." And so it was. But in keeping with the saying, "Trust God to move your mountain, but keep on digging," it was a miracle worked with the help of some very down-to-earth strategy and tactics.

TACTICS ON THE GROUND

The first thing the Helpers do when they speak to a woman contemplating abortion is tell her what her child will look like (a) after being crushed to death, and (b) after being sucked out of the womb. A photographic display, realistic enough to attract attention, but not so graphic as to repel, is laid out on the ground, rather than at eye level, since most women bent on taking the life of their child are too depressed to look up.

Into the hands of the woman goes a blue flier that speaks to her heart, as well as her head. On the front cover are the words, "Pregnant? Worried? We'll Help!" followed by a list of neighborhood pregnancy crisis centers that offer financial, as well as psychological and medical aid. The flier continues:

> How we can help you: free pregnancy test; free
> ultrasound; counseling as needed with parent,
> boyfriend, or husband; professional services (legal,
> medical, employment); spiritual support. We
> will arrange for housing and show you how you
> can continue with school. N.B. Our advice is
> strictly confidential and all our services are free
> – before, during, and after your pregnancy.

Next comes the "Did You Know" section revealing the risks of abortion (see Appendix B). Finally, there is the appeal:

Do you feel . . . . scared? Nervous? Alone? Angry? Frustrated? Overwhelmed? Do you wonder: how did this happen to me? What am I supposed to do now? Do you want help? Support? Answers? Who will listen and really understand how scared and sick and angry you are? **WE WILL**! You and your unborn baby are important, valuable human beings with basic rights and individual needs. **We care about you**. It is never too late to pray! Stop and ask Jesus to help you. He loves you more than you can possibly imagine. His power is greater than any problem, and He can heal any wound. He is waiting to help you. All you have to do is ask: "Dear Jesus, I am scared and I don't know what to do. Please come and be with me right now. Show me what to do and give me the strength to do it. Amen." **YOU ARE PRECIOUS IN GOD'S EYES**!

There are three things women will never learn from an abortionist: first, what he will do to their child to get it out of the womb; secondly, what the child will look like after it comes out; and thirdly, what kind of help is available. Those who enter an abortuary will never be urged to ask God for assistance. Nor will they be told, if they've already had an abortion, that a merciful Lord will forgive them provided they repent. On the contrary, hired "escorts" will hustle them into the clinic and try to relieve them, along the way, of any Helpers leaflets they may have taken.

PLEADING

Because Monsignor knows he will not have more than forty-five seconds, on average, to speak with a woman, he comes right to the point:

I walk toward the mother, Rosary and flier in hand, but I stop a short distance from her, so that she is coming to me, rather than I to her, and I try to appear relaxed and serene. Then I say, as gently as possible and with a smile, "Good morning, Mom. God bless you. May I speak with you for a minute — just a minute? I know you wouldn't be here if you didn't have a lot of problems — real problems." I tell her that help is available, — real help, and I explain the function of the various Life Centers listed on the front page of the flier giving a thumbnail description of the different types of aid, psychological, as well as material, all of it free. Then I say, "If the mothers don't get this help, the abortionist will go to work, crushing the child and turning on the suction machine for about four minutes to take the child out of the womb." As I am saying this, I pull out the "Did You Know" flier that shows the feet of the ten-week-old child and the results of suction machine abortion on a child of this age. "No matter how difficult things may be," I plead, "don't let anyone do this to your child."

At this point, I offer them a Rosary, putting it gently but firmly into their hands (otherwise, they are less likely to take it). At the same time, I give them a pamphlet on how to say the Rosary. Finally, I say, "If you need help yourself mom, please take this material. If you don't, please give it to someone who does. And watch out for the security guard. He is paid to confiscate this material because if the mothers use it, the abortion clinic loses money. Put it in your pocket — now." Sometimes, I give them an extra brochure and tell them to give one to the security guard while keeping the other for themselves.

It is important for women who have already had an abortion (50%) to know that the God of mercy never stops loving them, further that He is waiting for them to say "I'm sorry" and change their way of life. I tell them they need God's help. They need to pray; also that God will forgive them, as will their aborted child from his or her perch in heaven. "Those who have gone before you will rejoice," I tell them, "if you repent! The Lord will restore the body of your child; their soul is alive and well and with the Lord, Mom. It wants what the Lord wants, namely, for you to say you're sorry because it wants to see its mother again. If you are living with a fellow, you should have dumped the fellow, not the kid. He's got to stand by you. If he doesn't, he is not worthy of you."

If I have more time, I ask additional questions. For example, "Do you get to church? Do you pray? Are you Catholic?" If the answer to the last question is "yes," I go on: "Have you been to

confession? If not, you should go. Do you have
children? Are they baptized? Do you teach them
the catechism? Are you married? Were you married
in the Church? If not, get the marriage blessed."

Monsignor has too much confidence in his counselors to insist
that they memorize a script – his or anyone else's. He also knows
firsthand how exhausting their job can be. Turnarounds take time.
The seed sown by a Helper may never germinate, and if it does, it
probably won't happen until a woman is inside the mill facing staffers who are apt to be cold and impersonal: "How are you going to
pay? May I see your credit card?"

While Helpers are not easily discouraged, their task is not an easy
one. For every woman open to persuasion there are dozens who are
hostile. Which is why Monsignor tries to have at least two counselors
at every site. This way, when one of them needs some respite after
sustaining a series of brush-offs, he can oblige. No one is expected to
"succeed," either, only to do their best, because, in his words, success
presupposes "heroic virtue" and "tremendous generosity" on the part
of the mother (for a more detailed description of the Helpers method
see Appendix A).

THE VIGIL OF VIGILS

Going one-on-one with a woman contemplating abortion requires strategy, which is the theme of the present chapter. But there
is no better demonstration of Monsignor's skill as a strategist or tactician than his staging of the greatest prayer vigil of all time.

On June 13, 1992, John Cardinal O'Connor, the country's best-known churchman, led several thousand Helpers to one of New York's largest abortion clinics, a place where botched abortions had left two mothers dead.[2] The atmosphere was highly charged since O'Connor had given speeches from coast to coast as chairman of the U. S. Bishops' Committee for Pro-Life Activities, and he was not one to pull his punches, calling rescuers who blocked clinic entrances "heroes and heroines."

Over a steady drone of voices outside the church chanting, "Hail Mary, full of grace, keep it legal, keep it safe!" the Cardinal delivered a powerful homily recalling an incident in which a man had threatened to bomb the very clinic to which the Helpers were headed, Eastern Women's Center. O'Connor had made a televised appeal calling for the man to give himself up, and he told his listeners why: "We must never use violence to oppose violence."[3] Next, he mentioned a death threat he'd received the night before. There was laughter when he joked about the "pleasure" this might have given his auxiliary bishops; but the mood shifted quickly as he began to speak about a woman whom he knew personally. She had killed her child, turned to drink, and become a prostitute. But then, hearing him say on TV that he would never condemn a woman who aborted her baby, she was moved to penitence. She called to thank him, and a meeting followed in which he repeated Jesus' warning to the woman caught in adultery: "Has no one condemned you, neither do I condemn you. [But] go and sin no more!"

"I meet too many women," O'Connor continued, "some of them very young . . . who are confused, burdened, wearied, not knowing where to turn, desperate, pressured by friends and parents . . . How could I ever condemn such a woman, particularly when she sincerely believes she is doing the right thing?" Finally, he promised to under-write the cost of medical and/or legal services for any woman genu-inely in need, and it was a promise he kept.

Exposition of the Blessed Sacrament followed Mass, accord-ing to Helpers custom, and then it was five or six abreast down Lexington Avenue from 43rd to 30th street. As Monsignor's column filed out of the church, hundreds of pro-aborts began pointing their fingers and shouting "Shame! Shame!" One sign read, "Notre Dame for Choice."[4]

The situation, which had all the makings of a free-for-all, might well have turned ugly had Monsignor not been well prepared. Thanks to intelligence from a well-placed mole, he knew exactly what the protesters were planning. First, they would try to block the doors of the church to prevent his people from leaving. Secondly, they would rush the Helpers from opposite directions to break their column in two. Thirdly, they would lie down in the path of the procession in order to impede its progress.

For each of these moves, Monsignor had a countermove. A combination of parade barriers and mounted police was his re-sponse to plan #1 -- he would pin the protesters in place. To deal with plan #2 he had special security forces posted at key points along the flanks of the procession. His answer to plan #3 was a special agreement with the police. The moment he pointed his finger at any of the women sprawled on the ground, they would be arrested.

He knew that the protesters farthest from the Helpers were counting on being passed over, and so he deliberately singled them out, and once they were taken into custody, the rest simply melted away. In Monsignor's words, "it opened up like the Red Sea." There were eleven arrests, and when one of the women asked him why the members of her group were being arrested while Cardinal O'Connor's people were not, his answer was priceless: "Because you're not praying the Rosary and the Cardinal's people are!"

On arrival at the clinic, Reilly found police in riot gear guarding the entrance while about a dozen staffers wearing pink smocks escorted women in and out, covering their faces with sweaters or other clothing. Whenever the Helpers sang "How Great Thou Art" or some other hymn between decades of the Rosary, the pro-aborts would respond by beating drums and shouting "Not the church, not the state, women must decide our fate." Meanwhile, hundreds of whistling and jeering activists bombarded the Cardinal with insults and vulgarities.

Monsignor had instructed his people to refrain from reacting to the taunts. No one was to carry a sign. Leafleting was prohibited, and they were to "talk to no one, only to God." His marching orders were followed to the letter by nuns, priests, young couples, children, elders -- everyone. In addition, prayer marshals with red armbands helped folks recite the Rosary in unison.

Still, the atmosphere was rowdy. Every one of the six hundred police officers on duty was needed, and Monsignor made sure that the Cardinal, who wore a bullet-proof vest, marched some distance back from the front of the procession -- "barely visible in the knot of police and security guards that surrounded him" is how the papers described it.[5] Police cars rolled along on either side of O'Connor's entourage while four football stars, including all-pro tight end Mark Bavaro, took the lead. The 6'4" 245 lb. Bavaro said later that it was the scariest moment of his life!

After all was said and done, there was the usual flack. Pro-aborts claimed that the vigil reflected concern on the part of the Church that its campaign for the rights of the unborn was losing steam. "This is Cardinal O'Connor coming to the rescue," argued Frances Kissling, president of Catholics for a Free Choice. But naysaying aside, the 1992 prayer vigil, which set records in terms of participation and press coverage, was a huge plus for the pro-life movement, more significant even than what had happened in Los Angeles several months earlier under the leadership of Cardinal Mahony. The eyes of the world were focused on New York, a city where one out of every two children had been put to death since 1970; Reilly's tactical expertise was acknowledged far and wide; and a great many observers were encouraged to join the ranks of the Helpers.

On Sunday, the Cardinal's picture occupied the entire front page of *Newsday* and the *New York Daily News*. Even the *New York Times* took note:

> Because prayer – not confrontation – was the order
> of the day, the march signaled a departure from the
> strategy of anti-abortion groups whose civil disobedience
> tactics had not been successful in major efforts recently
> to close abortion clinics . . . . "We are here not to

condemn anyone," the Cardinal said during the hour-long Mass, "but to pray that on this day, a woman in any circumstance who feels pressured to have an abortion instead comes to us for all the love, support, and financial assistance she needs . . . . " "We've got to hold our tongues if we're going to set the better example," said Steven Fratta of Yonkers, echoing the words of Monsignor Reilly. "Jesus said, 'love your enemy.' People make mistakes; women have abortions. But we are all sinners. I didn't come down here to scream at women having abortions. I came down her to show my displeasure at a state that allows abortions."[6]

Skeptical reporters tried in vain to find a chink in Monsignor's armor. With his customary cool, he told them that "this type of witness asks everybody in America to think through their position -- those who disagree with us and those who agree. This [group of ours] is a cross-section of America, and they're saying, 'Look, we're going in the wrong direction.'"[7]

The day before the vigil, with his phone ringing off the hook, he agreed to a TV interview; but to guard against prejudicial editing and tape-splicing, he insisted that his remarks be aired live in their entirety. When Channel 9, with viewers up and down the eastern seaboard, agreed to his conditions, all seemed to be going well until the bell sounded for the actual show to begin. Then, out came the knives. "Why is the Church against abortion when a woman is the victim of rape?" they asked. Monsignor smiled, thanked them for the question, and let loose: "I have a good friend by the name of

Lauren, the pride and joy of her mother, who was conceived in rape. When Lauren came of age, her mother told her what had happened, adding that 'everyone I knew at the time advised me to kill you.' Do you want to support a procedure," Reilly continued, "that not only kills an innocent child in the womb and gives serious injury to the woman psychologically, but also lets the rapist go free by destroying DNA evidence of his guilt? The child is dead and the rapist escapes. Why should I fund this as a taxpayer? You want my friend Lauren killed? This is crazy!"

Monsignor knew he had scored because he had everyone in the studio applauding him by the time the session ended. Even the interviewers!

One more story regarding the 1992 New York vigil is a must since it is almost too good to be true. Monsignor received a message from the Cardinal on the preceding Thursday telling him to come to the headquarters of the Rockville Centre Diocese. O'Connor was staying there at the time and wanted to know what was being done to deal with threats of violence. Reilly had an answer, but he didn't receive the Cardinal's summons until well after mid-day and its tone was tough – he had to be at Rockville Centre by 4 P.M. or the vigil was off. With heavy traffic expected on the Belt Parkway, there was only one thing he knew for certain when he dove into his car and took off: he'd be cutting it close.

Then it happened. His vehicle began to shake, and it dawned on him that he was having a blow-out! Pulling onto the shoulder of the road and getting out of his car to assess the damage, he glanced at his watch. He'd never make it to Rockville Centre by 4 P.M.

Suddenly, there came a voice from behind asking, "Can I help?" When Monsignor explained where he was going, he was astonished at the response: "That's exactly where *I'm* going. Get in!" Climbing into a big beautiful car, he began praying to St. Anthony, whose feast day happened to coincide with the upcoming vigil. The driver must have sensed, from the way his passenger's lips were moving, that speed was of the essence, and so he stepped on it.

Weaving in and out of traffic like nothing Monsignor had ever seen, the driver managed to get him there in the nick of time. His watch showed 3:59 P.M. when the automobile ground to a halt. He had a whole minute to spare! But as he loped up the rectory steps, he realized that he hadn't asked the driver for his name! Down again he went. "What's your name?" he inquired. Came the answer: "Anthony." And with that, the mysterious personage drove off, never to be seen again.

CHAPTER 6

THE TEACHER

When Monsignor tells a story, it's usually because he wants to make a point, as in the case of his rescue by Anthony, which illustrates the power of prayer. Another of his instructive tales, one predicated on the idea that God helps those who help themselves, contains an appeal designed to involve parishioners in the work of the Helpers:

> Once upon a time, there was a man in need of
> money who prayed and prayed to God to let him
> win the lottery. Suddenly, he heard the gentle voice
> of God say, "Would you do me a favor and buy a
> ticket?" Folks, would you do *me* a favor and go pray
> with your bishop outside of the killing centers?

Still another story aimed at priming an audience for a desired course of action features a medical truck that pulls up at the side door of an abortion mill. The staff personnel, together with the truck driver, emerge from the mill with boxes containing the bodies of aborted children. The cartons, measuring a full fifteen feet in height, fully stacked, are thrown on the back of the truck and carted away with the rest of the garbage. Comes the appeal: "If our presence at the site saves one baby from being carted away in that truck, then God be praised."

These are the words of a man whose teaching career began very early. As captain of his high school basketball team, Reilly coached fellow athletes in the art of teamwork, and as a seminarian, he catechized inner city youths. At St. Teresa's, his students were the folks in the pews, and as an instructor on the faculty of Cathedral Prep, he taught Latin and chess, along with conduct (as dean of discipline).

None of this can compare, however, with his work over the past twenty-seven years. As head of the Helpers, he has shipped cassettes and videos, as well as copies of the magnificent Helpers *Prayer Book*, all over the world, oftentimes in translation. Workshops have been given at such schools as Marquette, Notre Dame, New York University, and Miami University of Ohio. Students from Franciscan University, Christendom College, and Catholic University have come on a regular basis to Brooklyn.

It matters not whether his audience is three hundred seminarians in Brazil, six hundred Nigerian girls in their teens, the Sisters of Life on retreat, or an international pro-life congress. His presentation will be enlightening, as well as inspirational. The prose is laced with attention-getting phrases such as "what happened was . . . " and "in other words." There are times, too, even in private conversation, when he will drive home a point by opening and closing the fingers of his hands with such velocity and force as to make a resounding smack.

THE USE OF CURRENT EVENTS

All of his newsletters begin with an education section, and moral lessons are drawn from current events. On one occasion, to illustrate the price of discipleship, he told what happened to a brace of heroes, one of them a Chinese priest who spent twenty-nine years in prison for loyalty to the Faith, the other an Omaha judge who resigned rather than issue a permit for abortion to a minor. When a reporter compared the judge's sacrifice to that of Thomas More, the latter hastened to set the record straight, "I only lost my job. Thomas lost his head."

The 9/11 attack on the World Trade Center was tailor-made for his technique. As he told it:

> The remains of the buildings were still burning as volunteer rescuers were searching desperately for any live bodies. As I prayed with closed eyes, the image I was seeing of innocent office workers unaware of their impending deaths suddenly gave way to the image of the unborn child at peace in the womb. Like the doomed souls inside the twin towers of the World Trade Center, the unborn child in the womb facing abortion goes about its everyday routine with no idea that the terrifying instruments of abortion are at hand and about to invade . . . . The terrorized child leaps, but there is no escape. The unborn child cannot understand what is happening, for only a minute ago life in the womb was as peaceful as it was for the people in the Twin Towers.

Ground Zero is being repeated every day in abortion "clinics" across America and around the world. Wherever you live, the unborn children plead with you to go to "Ongoing Ground Zero" where unborn children facing abortion need everyday heroes to rescue them. ... . The unborn plead with you to go to ground Zero near where you live. The unborn need you. They need your love, your presence, your prayers. Be rescuers. Be heroes. For the sake of the children, for the sake of the mothers and fathers and abortion staffs, for the sake of God.[1]

The war in Iraq was less gripping than what happened on 9/11, but it, too, was grist for the Reilly mill:

Our nation has rightly turned to prayer and fasting to end the war in the Gulf and bring our soldiers home safe. Should we do less to end the undeclared war against the unborn? War is not too real for us until we see on TV or in the papers the picture and name of a young man or woman killed in battle whom we know. The undeclared war against the unborn remains unreal for us because the unborn are destroyed before we can take their pictures or give them a name. A million a week! No words are adequate in the face of such evil.

When hostilities in the Middle East ended, Monsignor seized on the occasion to observe that "while we all rejoice and give thanks to God for the liberation of Kuwait and the end of the Gulf War, our joy is tempered by the tragic realization that the undeclared war against the unborn is far from over."

As a final case in point, when Pope Francis, during the Jubilee Year of Mercy, urged Catholics to engage in works of mercy, Reilly reminded his Helpers that they perform the spiritual works of mercy every time they go to the street:

(1) Instructing the ignorant – the Helpers sidewalk counselors offer information on where help is available to pregnant women; (2) Counsel the Doubtful – the Helpers will talk and pray with vulnerable women who doubt they can cope with a pregnancy; (3) Admonish Sinners – the Helpers do this in a loving way so that the woman will never return to the abortion facility, even if she chooses to destroy her child; (4) Bear Wrongs Patiently – the Helpers are constantly being harassed . . . . but [they] do not confront [their adversaries]; (5) Forgive Offenses Willingly – the Helpers are . . . at times, subjected to physical abuse without complaint; (6) Comfort the Afflicted – the Helpers will also reach out to any woman who has aborted her child to comfort and console her in her time of need; (7) Pray for the Living and the Dead – Helpers prayer warriors are constantly praying for both the mother and her child, [and] even if the child is not saved, the Helpers are praying for that child's soul. Many Helpers are also engaged with the corporal works of mercy, feeding the hungry, giving drink to the thirsty, clothing the naked,

and sheltering the homeless when they open their hearts
and wallets to help mothers who have decided for life.

If someone were to give me a dollar for every time Monsignor has
cited Scripture, I would be rich. When a disturbed woman shouted
expletives during one of his prayer vigils, he quoted Jesus: "Blessed
are you when they say all sorts of evil things against you for my sake,"
adding that since Christ was rejected by many in His life time, "we
should not be surprised or scandalized when we find that the teaching of the Church, through whom the Risen Christ continues to
bring His light to the world, is also rejected today by so many." Two
of his favorite verses, both of them from the Gospel of John, make
the same point: "He came unto His own and His own received Him
not" and "If they have persecuted me, they will persecute you" (1:10
and 15:20).

COSMOPOLITAN CREDENTIALS

Years of globe trotting have given him cosmopolitan breadth.
Without laying any claim to linguistic ability -- he gets by overseas with a smattering of European tongues – he has come to recognize the weaknesses, as well as the strengths, of America, and such
knowledge has served him well. By comparing the number of babies
aborted each year in Poland with the number aborted in Brooklyn –
252 vs. 50,000 – he was able to demonstrate, in easy-to-understand
terms, how far the people of his city had fallen. When Hungary
amended its constitution to ban abortion and "same-sex marriage,"
when Croatia minted a coin honoring the unborn child – all of this

served as a basis for comparison. Where was *our* movement for constitutional reform? Where was *our* pro-life coin?

When Russia's Putin outlawed abortion after three months and prohibited abortionists from advertising, the Helpers were treated to still another lesson: Eastern Europe, said Reilly, is "coming back from the dark sea of materialistic atheism into the safe haven of God and the world of the Spirit . . . the Eastern people who suffered so much in resisting the lie now know with greater clarity than the people of the West that the creature needs the Creator, and a fallen humanity needs a . . . Redeemer."[2]

PRIZE STUDENTS

One way to measure greatness in a teacher is to observe the effect of his teaching on others. Mother Agnes Mary Donovan, S.V. and Sr. Lucie Marie Vacile, S.V., founders of the Sisters of Life, discerned their vocation while praying with Monsignor outside one of the biggest abortion mills in the country. When Mother Agnes told him she might answer Cardinal O'Connor's call for a new religious order dedicated to the cause of life, he responded enthusiastically. A woman who served as Reilly's interpreter when he spoke at Vienna's center for life went on to found a religious order that brought the Faith to Russia's Pacific coast. His influence in such cases cannot be proven, of course, but the facts are suggestive.

Monsignor has trained pro-lifers by the hundreds. Some have spent months in Brooklyn learning how to counsel, launch post-abortion trauma programs, and build life centers. Dr. Catherine

Vierling, General Secretary of the World Movement of Mothers, was a guest at Precious Blood Monastery, as were Ana Garijo and Pintor Peiro, representatives of family movements in Spain. In the case of a couple from Mainland China, the husband and wife had been doctors before they ran afoul of Communist authorities. He landed in prison for refusing to perform abortions, while her punishment for defying the state was a hysterectomy. After escaping to Macao and making their way to the United States, they connected with the Helpers and were so impressed by Reilly's kindness that they volunteered to serve as photographers.

The day Fr. Emmanuel Ray Ikpa arrived from Jos, Nigeria, something really remarkable happened – remarkable enough to be recounted at length. Monsignor received an e-mail from a Nigerian woman in her fifth month of pregnancy who had been pressed by the child's father to have an abortion. When she refused to comply with the father's wishes, he left her, and the situation worsened after she lost her job. In Monsignor's words:

> I explained to Father Emmanuel the plight of the woman who said she was from the city of Abuja, and Father simply said to me: "Next Wednesday I am scheduled to fly into Abuja. I will try to help her." The woman gave me her telephone number in Abuja and I let her have Father Emmanuel's parish address and phone number.

> A few days later, at the end of one of the large prayer vigils, I introduced Father Emmanuel to those

attending and explained how God was providing for the woman through Father. The people at the Vigil spontaneously insisted they too wanted to help the woman by taking up a special collection. Immediately seven hundred dollars was raised which, given the favorable rate of exchange in Nigerian currency, was a huge sum. She received this financial aid from Father in Abuja on the following Wednesday! The difficult we do immediately; the impossible takes a few days! The woman has since written a letter of appreciation thanking the Helpers for their generosity and the concern shown her during her time of need. She said the funds helped pay for apartment rent and much-needed prenatal medical care.

The experience affected her so deeply that she now wants to help other pregnant women faced with sudden difficulty, and she will be able to do this since she is literate and skilled in the area of management. I told her the power of her good example has already helped a young woman here in Brooklyn who, on hearing her story, has decided to choose life for her child. Finally, on October 11 2005, I received a letter from the Archbishop of Jos, Most Rev. Ignatius A. Kaigama indicating that Father Ikpa has been entrusted with diocesan outreach to women with abortion-related problems. The Archbishop also said that if I wished to come to his diocese, he would be pleased to welcome me as his guest.[3]

Reilly lost no time accepting the archbishop's invitation. Abortion may have been illegal in Nigeria, but it was not uncommon, and his people helped to stave off legalization by erecting shrines to the unborn, conducting prayer vigils, and praying for the victims of back-alley abortions.

AMERICAN SUCCESS STORIES

Vierling, Garijo, Peiro, Ikpa . . . the list is long. Georgene and Matt Ulrich, after hearing Monsignor speak, sold their business to start a Helpers chapter in Seattle. Dan Goodnow, mentioned earlier, retired from an important job to launch the Helpers in Detroit.[4] David Bereit, another of Monsignor's pupils and the founder of Forty Days for Life, saw his movement spread to 500 American cities, along with nineteen foreign countries. Today, it claims 10,331 babies saved, 118 abortion workers converted, sixty abortion centers closed, and 650,000 praying and fasting for forty-day intervals twice a year for an end to abortion.

Joe Scheidler, the leading pro-life activist of Chicago, knew that Monsignor, in convincing some of the most hard-core abortion-bound women not to kill their babies, had converted dozens of mill workers. So he decided to bring five of his sidewalk counselors to Brooklyn, and when they arrived, they were taken to a killing center. Scheidler remembers a young Jewish woman, all in black, cursing Monsignor as she entered death's door, but coming out with her baby intact. Another woman dressed in leather and wearing an orange blouse entered the clinic, and Scheidler thought, "This gal -- no way." Ten minutes later, she, too, came out and gave Monsignor a hug. Still another girl dressed in a striped outfit was accompanied by a man. Although she yelled at Monsignor initially, she emerged from the mill fifteen minutes later seeking help. Said Scheidler: "I have seen the hand of God. I have witnessed the unfolding of a miracle. That day, thirty-seven pregnant mothers changed their hearts and chose life, one of them a Catholic who said she wanted to return to confession . . . . . [The presence of the Helpers] deprived the abortion industry of over $15,000 in fees."

Scheidler decided to change tactics: "In Chicago, we've saved thousands of babies from abortion using our Chicago method of sidewalk counseling," he wrote, "but now I want to incorporate the method developed by Monsignor Reilly . . . . to save even more women and their babies."[5] Which he did by flying Monsignor into Chicago to lead a field training exercise.

Dozens of additional names grace the Helpers honor roll. Dr. Jim Chu, a Yale University professor of aeronautical engineering who launched the Helpers in New Haven, was trained by Monsignor, as were some of the folks from Human Life International. Imre Téglásy, who spearheaded the outlawing of abortion and "same-sex marriage" in Hungary, runs the Helpers in Budapest.

Stojan Adasevic of Serbia, like Téglásy of Hungary, was never the same after meeting the founder of the Helpers of God's Precious Infants. Once the most notorious of child killers, he performed his last abortion after hearing Reilly speak. Pulling the hand of a well formed fetus out of the womb, he threw it on a marble table. Its nerves were not yet dead, and while he stared at it, the fingers moved. Next, he pulled out the heart of the unborn child and threw it down. It was still pumping. Then it stopped, and at that moment, all the lies about the unborn's lack of humanity, all the rationalizations he had concocted in performing 48,000 abortions, rang hollow. Suddenly, he saw the truth in all its clarity. "It's murder!" he shouted. Vowing never to do another abortion or counsel contraceptives (80% of which are abortifacients), he began organizing Helpers' prayer vigils, and today he runs the Life Center in Belgrade.

Dietmar Fisher, who directs the Helpers in Austria, served as Monsignor's chauffeur and translator before devoting himself wholly to the pro-life cause. Within a short space of time, his Life Center in Vienna had assisted 3500 pregnant women, and thanks to Fisher, there are prayer vigils today in all of Austria's major cities.

Abortion had been so common in Vienna that when one of the abortionists saw sixty university students on their way to his mill strumming guitars and singing lustily, he called the police. Officers were immediately dispatched. But because Monsignor had let them know in advance what to expect, they came to him first -- and apologized for being late!

There are so many fabulous stories about what the Helpers did in Austria, the hub of European pro-life activity, that one hardly knows where to begin. At one Viennese mill, prayer and counseling caused the entire staff to walk out. At another, the Helpers entered surreptitiously late in the day, and once inside, they examined the surgical equipment, heard Mass on the premises (celebrated by Monsignor), and left. Granted, this was not their usual mode of operation! But it worked -- the clinic closed. On another occasion, when Monsignor drove up to a Viennese convention hall to give an address, he saw hooded men standing outside the entrance and "WANTED" signs with his picture on them hanging from the lampposts. Police escort service was offered and accepted, no questions asked, and when Reilly registered at his hotel, he did so under an assumed name.

Need one say more? Cardinal Schönborn had it right when he told Bishop Daily that the Helpers "changed the face of Austria."

MARKS OF A TEACHER

Austria owes much of its change to a quality in Monsignor that I shall call "teacherliness," for lack of a better word. It is one part communication skill, one part mastery of subject matter, and a third part appreciating the good qualities of one's students. Monsignor qualifies on all counts.

Will Rogers, a popular entertainer of the 1930s, used to say that he never met a man he didn't like. Reilly may not come even with Rogers in this respect. I'm not sure he would *want* to. But one thing is certain: as a good teacher, he remembers names, bestows praise lavishly, and rarely forgets a Helper who is ill or deceased. Those who read back issues of his newsletters will meet Helpers who are "wonderful," along with priests who are "courageous." Monsignor's aides come across as "helpful," while Phil Moore, a nephew who runs the Helpers in Chicago, is "good and gentle." Most folks using such language would be written off as flatterers. But not Monsignor. He means every word of it. And what's more, it's true. Helpers' lay people *are* wonderful; the priests who support them *are* courageous.

As regards mastery of subject matter, Reilly has a firm grip on the fine points of reproductive science. But he is just as comfortable discussing history. Chosen to give the opening address for the 2010 World Congress for Life in Rome, his talk could have been superficial. Instead, it was an incisive summary of ideas and events leading up to the present crisis. Entitled "The Roots of the Culture of Death and Restoring a Culture of Life – or An Inhuman Humanism vs. a Christian Humanism," it began by noting the baleful influence of such thinkers as Thomas Hobbes (culture is nothing but self-interest and the popular will), Jean Jacques Rousseau (objective truth is merely what one can taste, see, smell, hear, and touch), and Karl Marx (economics explains everything, and man exists for the state).

Good ideas, observed Monsignor, result in good character and a culture of life, whereas bad ideas result in bad character and a culture of death: "By their fruits you shall know them. A good tree cannot bear bad fruit nor can a bad tree bear good fruit." The first "bad fruit" of the modern age, as outlined by Reilly, was Parson Malthus' late eighteenth-century prophecy that food shortages would bring an "overpopulated" world to the brink of starvation. The crisis that Malthus predicted never materialized, but the fear that it aroused remained to haunt succeeding generations. In 1968, Paul Ehrlich published a Malthusian best-seller entitled *The Population Bomb*. His argument was shredded a generation later by economist Julian Simon; but the mainline media never gave Simon's volume, *The*

Ultimate Resource (1981), the attention it deserved; and as a result, the myth of "overpopulation" marches on.

Next on Monsignor's list of "bad fruits" was Charles Darwin's theory of evolution or "survival of the fittest," which Nazi racists used to justify the sterilization of "inferior" people. The problem with this notion, as pointed out in the Rome speech, is that it fails to recognize races and cultures as complementary. Instead, it views them as competitors in a system where the weak and deformed, instead of being welcomed as a gift from God, are regarded as dead weight in a game of power.

The final portion of Reilly's talk dealt with feminism of the kind sold to a gullible public by eugenicist Margaret Sanger, the founder of Planned Parenthood. This was a woman who, by Monsignor's account, would have required a government permit for child bearing, a woman, moreover, who paid black ministers to promote contraception, who financed development of the pill, and who did all she could to ensure that American foreign aid, as well as UN assistance, would come with strings attached – strings requiring the promotion of contraception, sterilization, and abortion. Sanger convinced President Dwight D. Eisenhower that overseas population growth threatened American security, and, thanks to her lobbying, the President used foreign aid as a bargaining chip to pressure the leaders of countries that were poor.

Feminism of the Sanger sort turns women into slaves of the culture of death, mere instruments of sexual pleasure. Seen through the Sanger lens, men and women are competitive (as in evolution theory), rather than complementary, and human life ceases to be sacred. If human life is not sacred, then the procreative act that produces it is not sacred either, contraception becomes acceptable, and there is nothing wrong with *in vitro* fertilization or embryonic stem cell research.

True to the teaching of *Humanae Vitae*, Reilly warned his audience against deciding on the morality of an action without examining the full scope of its effect:

> When you say one can use a contraceptive because the world
> is overpopulated, you are only looking at the demographic
> part. . . . It is the same with marriage. We must look at the
> whole. We have to understand who man *is* in order to make
> a judgment about what he *does* . . . . Man is from God and
> is returning to God. He is made in the image and likeness
> of God. He must recognize who he is and what his nature
> is. Only then can he be what his creator intended him to be.

Monsignor went on to show that contraception, combined with abortion and sterilization, is a false answer to false problems fabricated by false prophets (Malthusians, social Darwinists, and radical feminists). Another "false answer" was Sanger's "Plan for Peace" which would have shunted millions of "unfit" Americans onto farms where programs of forced sterilization would benefit those who were "fit." According to Sanger, most forms of charity are cruel since they contribute to the survival of the "unfit."

By the time Monsignor reached the end of his Roman *tour d'horizon*, he had revealed the deadly thrust of both the Eisenhower administration's Draper Report and the Nixon administration's

National Security Study Memorandum #200, which sought to address "overpopulation" by requiring artificial birth control initiatives from less developed countries under the gun of international communism in return for U.S. economic and military assistance. His listeners also learned all they needed to know about Lyndon Johnson – that he appointed a Malthusian to head the United States Agency for International Development (AID), that he pressed the United Nations to give special aid to governments willing to introduce programs of population control, and that he got what he wanted -- by unanimous vote of the General Assembly.

WE WANT TO TEACH, WE WANT TO BE TAUGHT

One final product of Monsignor's "teacherliness" worth mentioning is his promotion of a plan to improve homilies. When the Second Vatican Council ordered that the standard catechetical sermon be replaced with one focusing on the Scripture reading of the day, the switch seemed harmless at first. But within a decade, young people no longer understood the Faith well enough to defend it. "What a shame," observed Monsignor in 2015, "we've just had a year of faith. What does that mean? Nothing. Much ado about nothing! It was meaningless because people don't know their faith. And if they don't know it, how can they spread it?"

Many homilies in the wake of Vatican II were nothing but a summary of the epistle or Gospel. Hence the name of Reilly's proposal for homiletic reform: "We Want To Teach; We Want To Be Taught." If adopted, priests the world over would devote the twenty-six Sundays of Ordinary Time to familiarizing parishioners with the *Catechism* in its abbreviated, compendium form. The first third of the *Catechism* would be covered during the first year, the second during the second year, and the third during year three. Scripture readings would be chosen to fit the homily, instead of the other way around.

Reilly sent his schema to the American bishops, as well as to the Vatican, and Benedict XVI seemed interested. But just as Cardinal Arinze, prefect of the Congregation for Divine Worship and the Discipline of the Sacraments, was about to take the proposal under consideration, he was forced to retire due to age. Pope Francis has received copies of the proposal in both English and Spanish. But it is unclear, as of this writing, what will come of it.

CHAPTER 7

THE THINKER

In our previous discussion of "teacherliness" we could have mentioned Monsignor's economy of expression and examined his stance on hot-button issues. But these subjects are weighty, and if we are to give them their just due, a separate chapter is needed.

For those of you who may wonder why we are concerned with economy of expression, the answer is simple. It is pedagogically important. A good teacher knows how to get to the point. Take, for example, the way Monsignor explains why God permits evil: "so tremendous goodness and holiness may arise out of it."[1] Ask him about freedom and he will tell you that there are many kinds, some good, some bad, most in need of limitation: "Your freedom of motion ends where my nose begins."

His description of a theologian's duty is equally terse: "to accept in faith the Church's official teaching and use his or her intellect to try and show why it is reasonable."[2] Two words were all he needed to describe the effect of papal ambiguity on moral issues -- "a disaster" -- while three sufficed to question a cardinal's agreement to serve as the grand marshal of a St. Patrick's Day parade in which

gays were permitted to march under their own banner -- "he blew
it" (meaning that he squandered a heaven-sent opportunity to clarify Catholic teaching on the difference between mere homosexual
attraction, which need not be sinful in and of itself, and sodomy).

His description of the news blackout that occurs every January
on the aftermath of the March for Life is vintage Reilly: "Beyond bias
to actual obstruction of truth."[3] As for *Roe v. Wade*, the judicial decision that, in his words, "sentenced unborn babies by the millions to
a horrendous death," it was "the end of civilization." But since *Roe*
is the very reason for the Helpers' existence, he naturally has more to
say on the subject:

> Flawed leaders, by misusing such words as freedom,
> choice, and equality, have anesthetized the people into
> passively accepting the removal from the laws of the land
> all Judaic and Christian values. The justices [in legalizing
> abortion] are defending fornication and contraception
> because, without abortion, the former would not be
> workable in many cases. In its 1992 *Casey v. Planned
> Parenthood* decision, the Court admitted as much. It could
> not muster a majority for the view that *Roe v. Wade* was
> correctly decided. Yet the majority insisted that even if
> the decision was wrong, it must stand because Americans
> had chosen a lifestyle (i.e. fornication and contraception)
> that depended on the availability of abortion.
>
> This ruling has helped create an abortion culture in
> which many Americans turn to the destruction of

innocent life as an answer to personal, social, and
economic problems. Which encourages many young
men to feel no sense of responsibility to take care of the
children they helped to create and no loyalty to their
child's mother. At the same time, men who do feel
responsibility for their children are left helpless to protect
them. The casualties from the Culture of Death include
not only the unborn but also the countless thousands
of women who have suffered physically, emotionally,
and spiritually from the deadly effects of abortion.
Fathers, grandparents, siblings, indeed entire families
suffer and are forever changed by the loss of a child.
The principles of *Roe* and *Doe* have also been used to
call into question the right to life of newborn children
with disabilities and adults with serious illnesses.[4]

Our government wants to take on [Middle East dictators]
. . . . Who is the threat to whom? We should clean up
our own house first . . . . Unless there is a massive moral
conversion back to Judeo-Christian ethics, you will
not need to ask for whom the bell tolls. It will toll for
you. . . . . Before the fifth commandment was broken,
the sixth and ninth were shot. We have to challenge
people to change their direction. They must know that
God loves them unconditionally. It doesn't matter if
we are deaf, blind, or retarded. It's all God's creation,
and God loves what He has made. The idea that a
child has to meet standards in order to live is absurd.
Whatever sacrifice has to be made should be made.[4]

Reilly rejects out of hand the argument that abortion is acceptable owing to its legality: "Evil is evil and good is good whether the law permits it or not. You cannot make evil good by legislating it. Neither can you make good evil by making it illegal. . . . right is right even if everyone is wrong." Once, when someone complained in a letter to the editor of *The Tablet* that the paper was devoting too much space to the pro-life movement when "every day, forty thousand children die of malnutrition," Reilly shot back: "That is a tragedy that needs to be remedied while not neglecting the greater tragedy of abortion. Greater? Yes, greater! Based on the most conservative estimates, each day in the world, 140,000 children are slaughtered by abortion."

Nothing over the years has saddened Monsignor more than the failure of church leaders to bring pastoral policy on Holy Communion into line with their condemnation of abortion. Two weeks before his founding of the Helpers, he wrote a strongly worded letter to the National Conference of Catholic Bishops. "Fellows," he began, "smell the flowers. We can't always be popular! Allowing pro-choice Catholic politicians to receive Holy Communion is sacrilegious. It undermines the sacredness of the Eucharist. If abortion is an infamous crime against humanity; if it is the ultimate discrimination against an individual by denying the person's right to life, then pastoral practice must reflect this clearly. Total fidelity to the truth always proves to be the most practical pastoral policy."

By way of practical advice, Reilly had the following suggestions:

Proposal #1: Every Saturday of the year should be
declared a day of prayer, penance, and reparation

as long as innocent preborn babies are legally being killed. Why Saturdays? This is the busiest day of the week for the death chamber abortion clinics who each year perform over 89% of the one and a half million abortions in our country. Since most of the killing for the week stops at about 3 PM on Saturday, church bells could be rung slowly for the preborn who have died that week. Especially at that time, 3 PM, prayers of reparation that would include asking God's mercy on doctors and mothers and lawmakers involved, etc. could be recited by God's people throughout the state. Everyone would be asked to give public witness by stopping whatever they are doing at 3 PM on Saturday and spending a few minutes in silent prayer concluding with a Hail Mary. Eventually, everyone would become acutely aware of the killing that unfortunately we, as a society, keep putting out of our consciousness.

Proposal #2: Any lawmaker who calls him or herself Catholic yet publicly votes for the legalization of abortions performed either by medical procedures or using mechanical or chemical abortifacients or any lawmaker who advocates the funding of abortion or prevents its restriction, such a lawmaker may not receive the Eucharist until he or she publicly ceases active involvement against the unborn.

Communion should be the moment and place where our spiritual oneness with Jesus and all those

united to Jesus is intensified. A person receiving the
Eucharistic Christ identifies with the victimhood of
Jesus by entering into communion with his life-giving
death. The act of abortion that deals death to life is
the total contradiction to the reality of the Eucharist.

Normally, no one wants the moment of Communion
to be a time of confrontation. Nevertheless, bishops
especially have been entrusted by Jesus with stewardship
over the Eucharist. If certain persons are not challenged
in light of what they do publicly, distribution of
the Eucharist becomes not confrontational but a
scandalous contradiction that either undermines
recognition by the faithful of a great evil or lessens
their awareness of the reality of the Eucharist."

Nine years after Reilly submitted his recommendations, the
American bishops issued the following declaration:

No public official, especially one claiming to be a faithful
and serious Catholic, can responsibly advocate for or
actively support direct attacks on innocent human
life. . . . Catholic political officials who disregard
Church teaching on the inviolability of the human
person indirectly collude in the taking of innocent
life. . . . . We urge our fellow citizens to see beyond
party politics, to analyze campaign rhetoric critically
and to choose their political leaders according to
principle, not party affiliation or mere self-interest.[5]

It was a milk-and-water statement, at best a half loaf, and when nothing was done to follow up on it, Reilly warned that "God will justly ask each of us what we did to prevent the innocent unborn child from being unjustly killed because the so-called 'private' act of abortion cannot take place without the cooperation of the whole of society."[6]

Among those cited by Monsignor as complicit in abortion were: anyone who rents space to the abortionist; anyone who makes the instruments used in the procedure; anyone who allows its advertisement (e.g. the Yellow Pages or a newspaper like *El Diario* in New York); anyone who passes laws allowing it; judges who find the law constitutional; those who work in the mill; those who bring others to the death chambers; those who enforce the law (the police); tax-payers who pay for Medicaid abortions; and finally, religious leaders who withhold the truth from the man in the pew.[7]

New York City came in for the harshest criticism:

> What a staggering accountability to God and History is
> ahead for this city and we who live here . . . When our time
> of heavenly judgment comes, and come it will, God will
> ask, "What did you do to protect my children?" Can you
> imagine telling Him: "Nothing, because I was pro-choice'
> or, even worse, 'Nothing, because I just didn't care!"[8]

THE STATE OF THE NATION

As a mourner of the kind described by Jesus in the Beatitudes (Matt 5:4) Monsignor laments the fact that our country is evolving into a tyrannical judicial oligarchy with the state "inside the sanctuary of the Church trampling on the religious conscience of the faithful." As he sees it, nine jurists have separated freedom from truth by removing from the law any values based on the Law of Nature as affirmed by the Declaration of Independence: "We hold these truths to be self-evident [i.e. Natural Law], that all men are created equal, that they are endowed by their Creator with certain unalienable rights, that among these are the right to life, liberty, and the pursuit of happiness." The law of the land must change, he says, but if faced with a choice between trying to change hearts and trying to change the law, he prefers the former:

> We want the law to change, but we don't want to
> force such change, because, even if the legalization of
> abortion were to end — and we hope it does — this
> would not be the end of our problem because there
> are a great many abortion mills in countries such as
> Brazil where abortion is illegal (except in cases of rape
> and danger to the life of the mother). In 1998, there
> were more abortions in Brazil than in the United States
> in spite of legal restrictions. . . . We have to change
> hearts, and to do this, we must pray, fast, practice
> virtue, and be present at modern-day Calvarys. Those
> who see us and hear us must be seeing and hearing
> Christ. . . . When abortion was illegal in Australia,
> the Helpers were still subject to withering ridicule,
> and it was the same in the United States during
> the years preceding *Roe v. Wade*. Abortionists were

active in many states, and those in authority turned
a blind eye to what was transpiring in back alleys.

THE SCHOLAR

Expect the man who taught Latin for twenty-six years at
Cathedral Prep to lapse into the tongue of Caesar on occasion and
even to bring in etymology. I found him remarking, for example,
on the irony of the word "euthanasia" -- it is derived from the Greek
for "good death." Drawing upon the wisdom of the ancients, he
will cite Marcus Tullius Cicero as a role model and quote from Peter
Canisius: "If you have too much to do, with God's help, you will
find time to do it all." Names like Churchill crop up regularly in his
newsletters, and if you look carefully, you will discover the words of
an illustrious nineteenth century poet: "When all its work is done,
the lie shall rot." What I remember best is a tribute to Gandhi:

> Seventy-five years ago, when a young, married man whose
> wife had become pregnant from an adulterous act was
> being pressured by his family to have the unborn child
> aborted, he turned for wisdom to Mahatma Gandhi. The
> wise man replied: "The essence of goodness is: preserve
> life, promote life, help life to achieve its highest destiny.
> The essence of evil is: destroy life, harm life, and hamper
> the development of life" . . . . Gandhi said further, "It
> seems to me clear as daylight that abortion would be
> a crime. It would be the sacred duty of the husband
> [should he discover that his wife is bearing the child of
> another man] to bring up the baby with all the love and

tenderness that he is capable of. Nor should I see anything
wrong in his accepting her repentance if it is sincere
and genuine and taking back the erring wife. Especially
since countless husbands are guilty of the same lapse as
this poor woman, but nobody ever questions them."[9]

THE ART OF COMPARISON

One of the factors in Monsignor's success as a communicator is
his deftness in drawing comparisons. We've already noted his use of
current events for the purpose of illustration. But it goes far beyond
the harnessing of news. Prayer, for instance, is likened to the human
heart – "not fully appreciated until it stops beating." A comparison
is likewise made between Al-Qaeda, which trains people to kill, and
city hospitals where doctors learn how to do abortions in order to
obtain their degrees. Abortion is dubbed "the ultimate child abuse,"
a "training ground in terrorism," even as what takes place every day
at abortion mills is analogized with what happened twenty centuries
ago at Calvary, where Innocence Incarnate was put to death.[10]

In one of the most instructive of all Reilly's parallels, the
denial of rights for the unborn is set alongside the situation with
slaves before the Civil War because, in both cases, injustice led
to violence. Since Monsignor's view is identical with that of
Dr. Nathanson, I will quote from the latter's autobiography, *The
Hand of God*, which is about as penetrating an analysis as one is
likely to find:

Not since the slavery issue and the rise of the abolitionist
movement has there been a comparably combustible

cultural war in this nation. In the run up to the Civil
War, there was . . . a decades-long string of increasingly
frequent and violent incidents. The pro-slavery side
got its licks in early and often, from the mob murder of
abolitionist journalist-minister Elijah P. Lovejoy in 1837 to
the near fatal caning of Charles Sumner by Preston Books
on the floor of the Senate in 1856. [But] as the prewar
conflict evolved, it was the fanatics among the abolitionists
who often initiated the violence, from Unitarian minister
Thomas Wentworth Higginson's two attempts in 1851
and 1854 to forcibly release fugitive slaves from federal
custody to John Brown's deadly raid on a pro-slavery
village on the Pottawatomie Creek in Kansas and his
suicidal attack on the federal arsenal at Harper's Ferry,
Virginia, in 1859, which culminated in the deaths of two
of Brown's sons and his own hanging six months later.

Although there are many superficial dissimilarities
between the questions of abortion and slavery,
there is one core issue at the epicenter of these
struggles common to both: the definition in
moral terms of a human being and the sweep of
natural rights that accompanies that status.

In the case of slavery, that issue was sharpened to a
razor's eye and brought unbearably on point by the
U.S. Supreme Court's 1857 *Dred Scott* decision, which
declared blacks, in effect, nonhuman, property. Free or
slave, said Roger B. Taney, the chief justice of the Court

who wrote the majority opinion, blacks could not be
citizens of the United States and therefore could have
no legal standing before the Court. Further, he wrote,
"Negroes are so inferior that they had no rights which a
white man was bound to respect," and then went on to
liken the slave, as pure property, to a mule or a horse.

Taney, [by] attempting to remove the issue from political
debate, radically constricted the possibilities of compromise
or discussion . . . . and may have made the war inevitable.

Are we marching down that same bloodied road in
the abortion conflict? . . . Like *Dred Scott, Roe v.
Wade* attempted to remove the abortion decision from
politics and thus effectively radicalized the debate,
discouraging compromise . . . . The declaration that
abortion was for all practical purposes an inalienable
constitutional right left pro-lifers unable to work
the political trenches at the state level or to push for
statutory restrictions at the congressional level. They
were left with only two options, one largely illusory.

Politically, they could pursue a constitutional amendment
banning abortion. But as more pragmatic pro-lifers have
repeatedly pointed out, the Human Life Amendment,
as it is known, is an exercise in quixotic futility. In the
absence of a national moral consensus on the issue, it is
simply too large a step to be the first step. An America

capable of passing a pro-life amendment would not need one; an America that needs one cannot possibly pass it.

Nathanson could have taken his analogy a step further by pointing out that many who defended slavery in 1860, like many who support abortion rights today, were liars. Here, as a basis for comparison, is what John Quincy Adams, Massachusetts Congressman, one-time president and unrelenting foe of human bondage, had to say about the slavery lobby in the years leading up to the Civil War: "Falsified logic, falsified history, falsified constitutional law, falsified morality, falsified statistics, and falsified and slanderous imputations . . . . All is false and hollow."[11]

This is not to suggest that the comparison between the 1960s civil rights movement and today's battle for the rights of the unborn is perfect in every respect. In the first place, the pro-life movement began relatively recently (in 1973 with *Roe v. Wade*), as compared with Martin Luther King's desegregationist cause, which had roots running deep in American history – all the way back to Reconstruction following the Civil War when racism and "Jim Crow" laws remained in place in many areas of the old confederacy.

Secondly, Dr. King had a huge constituency— practically the entire North, Midwest, and western region of the country, along with the reconstructed South. Almost all of the English-speaking world from Canada and England to Australia and New Zealand was on his side, not to mention the mainline media. Compare this with Monsignor's upstream swim against the current of political correctness.

CAUSE FOR CONCERN

Ask Reilly why America is in moral free fall, and he will tell you that its people have severed the three most important ties binding them to God: truth, goodness, and beauty. In their refusal to rise above themselves, they have replaced the joy of beauty with shallow fun and entertainment. Reverence, obedience, and gratitude – all are foreign to them because they refuse to shuck off their pride.

Modern man, mindless of where he stands in the order of things and usurping God's place as the arbiter of right and wrong, sees himself as "entitled to shorten the lives of others by euthanasia." He contracts marriages and gets divorced the way he "exchanges one glove for another." Instead of seeing children as a gift from God, he "plays God by determining their number." Unable or unwilling to admit the existence of Divine Providence, he seeks to "replace the rhythm of a truly human life with insurance against things unforeseen and unforeseeable."[12]

Blind to the tragedy befalling him, he is like a frog in a pot of water. There is fire under the pot, and as the temperature gradually rises, he can jump out. But he doesn't. And so he boils to death.

A similar observation was made some years ago by the late Archbishop Fulton J. Sheen:

It is a characteristic of any decaying civilization that
the great masses of the people are unconscious of the
tragedy [befalling them]. Humanity in a crisis is generally
insensitive to the gravity of the times in which it lives.
Men do not want to believe their own times are wicked,
partly because they have no standard outside of themselves

by which to measure their times. If there is no fixed
concept of justice, how shall men know it is violated? Only
those who live by faith really know what is happening in
the world; the great masses without faith are unconscious
of the destructive processes going on because they have lost
the vision of the heights from which they have fallen.[13]

Once the cancer of sin metastasizes and a nation loses its
moral fiber, there is nothing, including "same sex marriage," that
is not accepted. When Daniel Murphy, home run hero of the
New York Mets, was asked in a postseason interview what he
thought of a fellow player who had "come out of the closet" as a
homosexual, he replied, "My religion doesn't accept [it] . . . I'm
against it." Although Monsignor is a die-hard Yankees fan, his
reaction to Murphy's statement left no doubt as to where he stood:
"He [Murphy] came right out [with it]. No apologies. . . . . The
Church, [which is] weak in teaching these things, has to say 'no' to
the state."[14] Murphy was simply saying that, as a Catholic, he believed sodomy to be wrong, and it was for trying to state the truth
about his faith (even though he didn't distinguish, as he might
have done, between mere homosexual attraction and sodomy) that
Monsignor commended him.

Rare nowadays is the clergyman who will remind Catholics of
their obligation to square off against the evil of contraception -- the
silence emanating from the pulpit is deafening. But Monsignor
comes right out with it: "To plan convenient pregnancies and decide
exactly how many children fit into their life plan rather than letting
God do His will [is wrong] . . . . Human love must never deliberately

exclude the creativity of God, which brings forth . . . a human being who is to exist forever." Uudeterred by the dictates of political
correctness, the man from Precious Blood Monastery points out that
separation of the unitive and procreative purpose of sex opens the
door to "same-sex marriage," even as use of the term "meaningful
life" by contracepters and abortionists suggests that the lives of children born with Down Syndrome or elders plagued with Alzheimer's
may be meaning*less* and therefore expendable.[15]

GOOD CHEER

On the one hand, Monsignor has never shrunk from sounding
the bugle for Catholic action, and he can be fierce in his criticism.
On the other, his words, on balance, are wonderfully encouraging.
The same man who condemns the culture of death, maintains that:

> The vast majority of Americans, like their Founding
> Fathers, still believe in the laws of Nature and Nature's
> God . . . tremendous goodness and holiness is rising
> up out of this culture of evil and death . . . When God
> wants to move, He does . . . He has a plan, and we are
> part of it. Otherwise, He would not permit such evil.[16]

He won't pull his punches when it comes to the behavior of
Church leaders who fail to measure up to the highest standards, but
neither will he tolerate criticism of the clergy that is unjust or exaggerated. Acknowledging the shamefulness of Church scandal in
2010, his message to the press was nothing, if not positive:

These days, one would have to be blind or deaf not to read in the newspapers or watch on television the unrelenting attack by so many commentators against the Catholic Church, one that has been going on for years in the United States, and now, more recently, in Western Europe. One commentator went so far as to say, "This may be the end of the Catholic Church." I thought to myself, you foolish man. It is not the end of the Catholic Church, but rather of Western Civilization whose flawed leaders, by misusing words such as "freedom," "choice," and "equality," have anesthetized people into passively accepting the removal from our laws of all Judaic and Christian values. Without these ethical foundations, Western Civilization will collapse and perish. For it was moral values as found in God's Commandments and the recognition in law of the absolute value of every human life as created by God that made the laws in western civilization great and admired.

While most of the news over the past forty or fifty years has been discouraging from a pro-life standpoint, Monsignor remains upbeat. Frank Drollinger makes a good comparison between the Helpers and the embattled patriots of the American Revolution. The outcome of the War for Independence was far from inevitable, preceded, as it was, by the trials of Valley Forge. The Continental Army commanded by Washington numbered less than one percent of the population, and those who didn't fight were, for the most part, hostile or indifferent. But what counts is that the man from Mount Vernon never lost hope.

It is the same today. Reilly, like Washington, assures his follow-ers that "there is light at the end of the tunnel . . . good things are happening":

> a culture of life will be restored . . . The produce
> being sold from the tree of death is worse than
> rotten. It is deadly and is not only causing death
> to the weak and dependent, but grief and sorrow
> to the strong who survive. Obviously, the product
> can't sell without massive deceptive advertising.
> Many who have purchased it in the past will not
> recommend it, while others will publicly condemn
> it. Furthermore, many of those living in the so-called
> undeveloped world who are considered unfit to breed
> have had their eyes opened to the point where they
> can see the hook of death attached to the demonic
> aid of the West and so are refusing to accept it.

"Good Things Are Happening" is the title of Monsignor's theme song! Was he shaken when a tsunami following an earth-quake kept his plane from landing in Japan? Or when men dressed as policemen hauled him off a bus in Benin, forcing him to pay a phony fee and adding six hours to his trip? He came away un-fazed. Far from being down when a tornado diverted his plane from Chicago to Indianapolis causing him to miss an important engagement, he made light of it, secure in affirming that "just when everything seems to be going awry" the Lord "has the most wonder-ful things in store."[17]

Listen to his description of a nine-hour plane trip to Vienna:

My seat refused to go back, and the stewardess couldn't do
anything about it. To my left, there was a loud child who
kept me from sleeping. I decided to prepare my talk, and
what do you suppose? The overhead light went on the
fritz and remained that way for the duration of the flight!
I knew then that my trip was going to be a great success.

And it was! A huge crowd turned out to hear him speak.

The same thing happened in the Ukrainian city of Kiev.
Lodged in a house without running water or electricity, he had to
mount a ladder at night and climb through a hole in the ceiling
to reach his bed, which turned out to be too short for his 6'1"
frame. This is all it took for him to be certain that his mission
would succeed. Toward the end of one of his speeches, when the
time keeper handed him a three-minute warning, thousands of
listeners rose up and began shouting, "No! No! Let him speak!"
Speak he did, the only one on the program permitted to exceed
his allotted time.

Again and again, Providence has seen him through. There was
the time when a pro-abort woman shouted to him on the street,
"Stop your praying and do something useful. Go out and raise
money to give to pregnant women in need!" Monsignor kept on
praying, and moments later, the driver of a big black car pulled
up and rolled down his window. Giving one of the Helpers what
looked like three one-dollar bills, he said, "Use the money for the
women in difficulty and keep on praying!" The bills turned out

to be *hundred-dollar* bills. And not only this. The woman who berated the Helpers never saw the car or the driver; neither was she seen or heard by the driver.

On another occasion, Monsignor was in Auckland, New Zealand, headed for a speaking engagement in Melbourne, Australia, when he found that he needed a visa. It meant flying to Wellington, which was far out of his way. But trusting, as usual, that something good would come of it, he ran headlong into Wellington's archbishop, who put him up for the night and was so taken with the work of the Helpers that he became a sponsor. The next day, Reilly missed his flight to Melbourne due to overbooking. But on returning to the archbishop's residence, he found all of New Zealand's bishops on hand for a conference. He offered them promotional packets and found them as receptive as the archbishop! "When God changes your plans," says Monsignor, " it's always for the best. He changes mine quite often."

THE BEST ANTI-DEPRESSANT

Monsignor's sense of humor is the best anti-depressant on the market. When he recruits sidewalk counselors, he tells them that "the pay is not much, but the benefits are out of this world." Meanwhile, for those who are less than pleased with the editorial policy of the *New York Times*, he suggests that the paper change its motto from "All the News That's Fit to Print" to "All the News That Fits."[18]

Although humor in its classic sense is meant to delight and instruct, it can also be used as a weapon in self-defense. One Saturday, when the Helpers turned out early to pray and sing at an abortion mill in liberal Iowa City, a man upbraided Reilly for disturbing late sleepers. "The gentleman did not understand," Monsignor rejoined, "that we were there precisely to make sure that the unborn children's sleep was not disturbed."

Finally, if you want a good laugh, listen to what happened when Monsignor's flight from Albuquerque, New Mexico, to Tuscon, Arizona, was cancelled. He told his host, Ed Ryan, about it and Ed said, "Don't worry. I'll find you something else." The "something else" turned out to be a Great Lakes Airlines flight. "Great Lakes?" inquired Monsignor, "in the middle of a southern desert?" "Yes," said Ed, "they're here and they fly to Tucson. Worry not." After clearing airport inspection, Reilly carried his bag to the last gate of the terminal and asked the woman at the counter, "Is this Great Lakes Airlines?" "Yes," she replied, "may I check your bag?" Unburdened, he began descending a flight of stairs onto the tarmac when he heard a loud banging. The person bouncing his luggage down the stairs behind him turned out to be the lady at the counter. "Was she the pilot, too?" he wondered.

Once all ten of the passengers were seated aboard the propeller-driven puddle jumper— five on either side of the aisle in single-file-formation — the pilot, who occupied a regular seat in front, said to them, "We'll never make it out of here without some weight redis-tribution" (the airport was surrounded by tall mountains; hence the need for a rapid gain in altitude after takeoff). He then asked each of them how much they weighed so he could arrange the seating to ensure optimal flying efficiency. "I could hardly believe my ears,"

Monsignor chuckles. "Was this a joke? I pleaded with the other passengers, especially the ladies, to tell the truth about their weight! It
was a matter of life and death! Finally, the pilot says, 'OK. Let's give
it a try.'"

Laughing uproariously at the words "give it a try" and repeating
them for comic effect, Reilly goes on:

> As the puddle jumper labored down the runway and
> began its gradual ascent, people prayed as they'd never
> prayed before! You could practically reach down
> and pick the flowers on top of the peaks. That's how
> close we came. Then, when I got back to New York
> and glanced at a copy of the *New York Times*, what
> should I see but an article about Great Lakes Airlines!
> It was suspending operations because government
> inspectors had found its aircraft "unworthy."

Recently, I asked Monsignor if he made it to Tucson on time to
give his scheduled talk. "Absolutely," he replied with his usual buoy-
ancy. "It went really well, just as I knew it would when my original
flight was cancelled."

CHAPTER 8

THE DEFENDANT

The hostility of abortion providers and their allies is a given if you are pro-life. It "goes with the territory," as they say, and Monsignor has had his fair share. Sued for millions of dollars, he has had to make dozens of court appearances. Many are the times when his Helpers would have been stymied without swift and effective action on his part. Misguided police officers regularly take them to task for action that is perfectly legal. Time and again, the City Council has threatened to cripple their counseling. Time and again, Reilly has made appeals and gone through channels.

It's a good thing that he knows the law. He incorporated the Helpers as a non-membership organization consisting strictly of volunteers so that no one, with the exception of himself, could ever be sued. At the same time, he made sure that out-of-state chapters were separately incorporated -- his "hydra-headed monster," as he calls it. This way, an attack on one would not be an attack on all. If New York's courts were to do their worst, he could simply declare bankruptcy and start over.

When he heard that Helpers in other states were being charged for police protection, he discovered a 1992 Supreme Court ruling prohibiting such practice on the basis of First Amendment rights (*Forsyth v. Nationalist Movement*). Interestingly enough, the majority opinion for *Forsyth* was written by Harry Blackmun, the same judge who drafted the majority opinion in *Roe v. Wade* nineteen years earlier. As Monsignor says, "I used Blackmun to protest Blackmun." Out-of-state Helpers were briefed on the finding and told, in addition, how to deal with the media and apply for a parade permit.

Reilly has never lost out in his brushes with the law. Ask him why, and he'll tell you, "I have a good friend, the First Amendment." The First Amendment is indeed his friend, but the value of the friendship is due, in no small part, to the pro bono work of a Wall Street lawyer by the name of Kathleen O'Connell, who, as we saw earlier, drew upon her expertise in Constitutional law to ensure the Helpers' right to pray and counsel on public sidewalks outside the sites where unborn children's lives were being taken. Had her contribution been limited to professional advice, research, and legal briefs, it would have been invaluable. But she did a great deal more, pleading the Helpers' case in numerous court room hearings and representing them in meetings with police captains and City Hall politicians. If she had charged for her time, the cost would have been close to a million dollars in today's terms, far beyond anything the Helpers could afford.

THE HOLTZMAN BILL

In 1993, City Councilwoman Elizabeth Holtzman introduced a bill to prohibit "conduct that would alarm or intimidate a reasonable person" at abortion clinics. Monsignor feared that a pro-choice judge might interpret recitation of the Rosary or the picturing of aborted fetuses as "conduct that would cause alarm." And so he fought for an amendment that would define objectionable behavior in concrete terms as physical obstruction, damage, or intimidation. After months of negotiation, he prevailed. But three years later, he had to face the toughest legal challenge of all, a battle that would drag on for three years and require forty trips to court. Brooklyn's Ambulatory Surgery Center, mentioned earlier, in concert with the National Organization of Women and Planned Parenthood, sued the Helpers for 117 million dollars.

THE AMBULATORY LAW SUIT

Ambulatory was the biggest abortion provider in the city, occupying an entire city block. With four operating rooms, it was better equipped than most hospitals for killing. The plaintiffs claimed that the Helpers, in addition to beating on car windows, stalking clients, and reducing them to tears, had blocked, grabbed, pushed, and photographed women while shouting abusive language. The principal charge, however, was that by following women and speaking to them when they turned a deaf ear, Reilly's people were breaking the law. Especially damning was the witness of Peter Garda, a police officer who testified that he had told the Helpers about three times a week to "back off."

The first thing Ambulatory did was to apply for a temporary injunction against street counseling. Court orders of this kind tend to become permanent because the cost of fighting them is prohibitively high, and so Monsignor asked the police to pay careful attention to what was happening at each of the killing sites. This they did, and, as a result, they were able to give seven hours of helpful testimony, more than enough to forestall the issuance of an injunction.

In such situations, it mattered that Monsignor had a history of getting along with law enforcement officers. Police officers are on the side of the unborn child, at least in theory, because they are pledged to protect human life. At the same time, they don't like surprises, and with the Helpers there aren't any. Monsignor lets them know, in advance, where he is going, as well as what he plans to do, and he never crosses them. Even when they give the Helpers trouble and Reilly knows his people are in the right, he will yield and go through proper channels.

In dealing with Ambulatory, which was in league with Planned Parenthood and the National Organization of Women, it didn't hurt that Lester Paverman, the legal counsel for the Police Department, was a Catholic who respected Monsignor's interpretation of constitutional law. Helpful, too, was O'Connell's background as police Commissioner for Legal Affairs and professor of law at the Police Academy. Monsignor also had family connections. His father worked as a security guard. His uncle, who was also his godfather, made a living as a NYPD officer. Last, but not least, Detective Steven McDonald, who accompanied him on many of his prayer vigils and testified on his behalf at City Hall in his wheelchair with the aid of an oxygen tank, was a police officer from a family of police officers.

O'Connell began her defense by demonstrating that it was permissible under existing law to talk to unreceptive people on the street. For such action to be illegal, it had to arouse reasonable fear of physical harm, which was never the case with the Helpers. "Under the First Amendment," she argued, "the right to free speech may not be abridged simply because the listener expresses disinterest in what is being spoken; indeed, if the law required people to discontinue peaceful speech whenever someone expressed disinterest, then every salesman and political candidate in America would risk prosecution." Monsignor weighed in by adding that a distressed woman's "don't bother me" might not be indicative of her true feeling: "Quite often, people say 'no' before they understand what is being said to them. In fact, not long ago, a woman who had undergone an abortion told me that if she had understood what I was saying, she would have accepted my offer of help."

O'Connell won an early round by demonstrating that Garda's "back off" orders to counselors were the result of pressure from Ambulatory and out of line with practices in other precincts. The commanding officer of the 72nd Precinct testified that a search of police records had failed to turn up any arrests of Helpers or even any complaints -- no officer assigned to Ambulatory had ever filed an incident report. In addition, Garda made five important admissions under cross examination: (1) the Helpers never blocked entrances or shouted abusive language (i.e. "murderers!"); (2) there had been no forcing of leaflets on anyone -- nothing, in fact, but courtesy; (3) the Helpers had been totally cooperative; (4) if clients cursed them, they had backed away, saying, "I'll pray for you"; (5) there was nothing on the record to indicate that they followed people who said, "leave me alone."

One of Ambulatory's principal claims was that the Helpers, using bait-and-switch tactics, had made promises of financial and medical assistance that they didn't intend to keep. Patients were allegedly lured to a life center, only to be told on arrival that financial aid was unavailable except for a select few who "qualified."

Sr. Dorothy Rothar, CSJ, introduced earlier as one of Monsignor's most experienced sidewalk counselors, made quick work of the allegation. Yes, women had to qualify for assistance, she conceded. But what of it? Could they expect free medical care unless they were (a) pregnant, (b) uncovered by medical insurance, and (c) unable to pay? Citing New York State's P-Cap program which offered free prenatal care, along with payment for all medical bills and other services to both employed and unemployed working mothers whose income was as high as 185% above the income level required for Medicaid eligibility, she pointed out that most major hospitals participated in P-Cap and thus provided free prenatal care to low income women without proof of citizenship and without restriction as to age. "While I have referred hundreds of women to crisis pregnancy centers over the past few years," she said, "I know of no situation in which a woman who was financially unable to pay for proper medical care during pregnancy and delivery or proper neonatal care after delivery was deemed ineligible for P-Cap."

Not content with misrepresentation in the courtroom, Ambulatory hired a private detective to infiltrate the Helpers and thus incriminate them from within. When this didn't work, they faxed obscene song lyrics to O'Connell, thinking that such words as "shit" and "dick" might break her spirit. O'Connell turned the tactic on its head by labeling the missives "hate mail" and "vicious, anti-Catholic bigotry" that spoke volumes about the motives behind "the plaintiffs' frivolous, vexatious lawsuit."

The high point of her defense came when she proved, on the basis of research conducted at the Board of Elections and U.S. Bankruptcy Court, that signatures and notarizations on eleven of Ambulatory's affidavits were phony. Thus was she able to dismiss the case for the prosecution as "no more than an intemperate tirade filled with invective and baseless accusations":

> The plaintiff's counsel has outdone himself in cheap tactics in an attempt to impugn the reputations of the defendants. He has secretly recorded conversations with Helpers, paid people to join the Helpers prayer group and filled the Court's files with irrelevant newsletters, even attempted to provoke an incident with the Helpers. They have claimed that someone "affiliated" with the Helpers threatened to blow up Ambulatory and everyone inside — typical of Plaintiffs desperation . . . In fact, NYPD records show that Ambulatory never reported such an incident, but rather that the threat reported was made by a drunken male talking incoherently as he walked by. The police know the man and know that he has no association with the Helpers.

Incredible as it may seem, the presiding judge at the State Supreme Court failed to acquit Monsignor — notwithstanding Ambulatory's admission of false signatures and notarizations! However, the case got bumped up to an appellate court where corruption was less of a problem, especially with Cornelius

O'Brien, a highly respected pro-life jurist, on the bench. Great was Monsignor's disappointment when O'Brien recused himself (because he and his wife had marched in Helpers' prayer vigils!). But joy followed when the five-member panel of lawyers that took O'Brien's place ruled 5-0 in his favor. It was a stupendous victory, long overdue, and although Ambulatory, Planned Parenthood, and the National Organization of Women (NOW) never formally dropped their lawsuit, they never pursued it either because they had been exposed for what they were, liars who had to pay a court-imposed fine for perjury.

THE FROZEN ZONE

As the prelude to another pitched battle of the 1990s, Choices abortion mill at Lefrak Center on Queens Boulevard persuaded the police to declare their sidewalk a "frozen zone." This had an immediate, negative effect on the Helpers because it forced them to retreat to a spot across the street. But when some of Monsignor's friends urged him to sue, he declined. "This is political, not legal," he told them, and what was the point of being tied up for years in court? Instead, he persuaded Cardinal O'Connor and Bishop Daily to authorize a statement to be read at all of the city's 600 parishes on a Sunday-to-be-announced. In essence, it accused Mayor Giuliani of preventing women from receiving important information, and once he had this under his belt, he requested a meeting with Giuliani, threatening, in the event of refusal, to go public with his statement.

Giuliani granted Reilly's request without delay. But when the meeting got under way, it was found that the mayor had a radical feminist at his side. This might have been daunting for anyone else in Monsignor's place, but for the man from Precious Blood, it was simply another move in the chess game of city politics. Taking care not to say anything about abortion or unborn children, he informed Giuliani that frozen zones, in addition to being unconstitutional, would deprive the women of New York of information they had every right to receive. Why, he asked, should they be treated unfairly?

Incredibly, the feminist flanking the mayor agreed with everything Reilly had to say. Giuliani promised to look into the matter, and that was the end of the matter. There were no further problems.

INTRO 465A

The victory was sweet, but short-lived. On August 21, 2001, the Public Safety Committee of the New York City Council held a hearing on whether to recommend legislation (Intro 465A) that would have imposed a ten-foot moving bubble around anyone within fifty feet of an abortion clinic. People coming within the bubble to protest, pass out information, display a sign, or converse with someone without their consent could incur a fine, jail time, or both; and the fines were stiff. For a first offense, the penalty would have been $1,000 and/or six months in jail; for a second, $5,000 and/or a year in jail. Conspiracy charges could also to be brought against anyone acting "pursuant to a common plan or design," raising the possibility that Helpers praying across the street, and even the priests who supported them, might be held accountable.

Intro 465A was draconian, going far beyond the city's 1994 clinic access law which made it a crime to physically block or harass patients or staff members on their way into or out of abortion clinics, and Giuliani was expected to sign it.

Fortunately, pro-lifers turned out in force for a legislative hearing. New York State Right-to-Lifers, members of The Catholic League, Holy Name societies, Knights of Columbus, and Hibernians -- all were there, outnumbering their opponents 4 to 1. Even the American Civil Liberties Union was there -- *on the side of the Helpers* thanks to Monsignor's squadron of angels.

In the course of the hearing, more than forty individuals spoke for and against the "Gag Rule," as the Helpers called it, with backers of the proposed legislation interrupting the proceedings with groans, boos, and derisive laughter. Things got so out of hand that the committee chair, after asking repeatedly for quiet, felt bound to admonish the crowd for a "self-defeating attitude" that showed lack of respect and might lead observers to conclude that this was the sort of behavior they could expect at a clinic. "That's your opinion," a man in the audience shouted back.[1] As if pro-lifers were the ones misbehaving!

Councilwoman Kathryn Freed, the bill's sponsor, maintained that buffer zones were "not an abridgment of anybody's freedom of expression," which was false. After claiming, again without foundation, that the Supreme Court had upheld a "similar" law in Colorado, she lied a third time when she told *Catholic New York* that police officers were shirking their duty. A new bill was needed, she alleged, in order to "clarify" the definition of harassment, which was being left too much to the discretion of the NYPD.

O'Connell was quick to deny the need for new legislation since harassment was already illegal under the federal FACE law and the New York Access to Reproductive Health Services Act (33A). Far from being needed to preserve what Freed called a "constitutionally protected right to choose," there was only one reason for the bill, O'Connell maintained, and that was profit since the abortion industry loses a surgery fee every time a woman says "no."[2] Could those, she asked, who supported the bill say exactly when the alleged incidents had taken place? Had they reported them to the police? Did the clinic operators have visual evidence of objectionable behavior on the part of the Helpers? She knew what each of the answers would be, and by the time the meeting ended, she had established three important facts: no complaints had been filed, no harassment had been proven, and there was regular patrolling by the men in blue.

She was loudly applauded when she noted that politicians routinely approach people on the street, handing out unsolicited literature: "The same council members who approach people on the street uninvited . . . are proposing a law to make it a crime for certain New Yorkers with pro-life beliefs to do the same thing."[3]

The other high point in the proceedings came when clinic director, Beth Loschin, charged Monsignor with "insensitivity to women." Monsignor held up a two-page spread-sheet from a recent edition of the *Daily News*. There in vivid color was a picture of Loschin and her boyfriend, James Warren, beside a caption identifying them as rapists and sex-traffickers who had lured a teenage girl into a car, handcuffed her, raped her, and loaned her out as a sex slave to one of their male friends![4] According to the exposé, Warren, who had spent three years in jail for abusing a child, had been accused by his own sister of sexual assault. "The effrontery!" thundered Monsignor. "These people are accusing *me* of insensitivity to women?"

Reilly's appeal to the Council deserves to be read in its entirety:

Good morning, Mr. Speaker and members of the Council.
I am Msgr. Reilly, the President and Executive Director
of the Helpers of God's Precious Infants. I stand in
prayer, outside of abortion clinics in this city each day
for five or six hours, praying for the conversion and
salvation of all those having or performing abortions.
I pray and speak and offer help to the mothers who
come each day to these clinics. I know that the moms
have real problems or they wouldn't be coming here.

I also know that well-meaning people tell these women
that abortion will solve their problem by restoring
yesterday. As a priest for forty-one years who has spoken
to thousands of women who had abortions I am convinced
abortion does not bring back yesterday but rather destroys
for moms the peace of tomorrow. As soon as the womb is
empty, mom's head and her heart are filled with pain and
I want to be there with the compassion and forgiveness
of Christ. I speak to women before an abortion and after
an abortion. It is obvious you don't convert or touch

the heart of a person by harassing or intimidating them. The Helpers always try to establish a loving, prayerful presence which will open the hearts of mothers to the help we offer them. They are always treated with respect and dignity even if they have the abortion. We don't need a law to do this; the Helpers do it as a matter of policy.

In spite of the Helpers' peaceful policy . . . [you have no idea] how many false charges good citizens, praying and counseling on public sidewalks, have had to face. For the past three and half years, Dr. Michael Levy and his administrators Beth Dixon and her successor, Francis Xavier Monck, have tried to get a court-ordered injunction that would impose a 50 foot buffer zone not only on myself, but also on Bishop Daily, the Bishop of Brooklyn, and all the good citizens who come to pray or counsel on the public sidewalk outside the abortion clinic.

These past three years have been painful because of the unrelenting series of false charges brought by abortion providers to the media, to the FBI, and to the NYC Police Department. Every one of them has been investigated and rejected as without foundation. As a result, just recently, the New York State Appellate Court not only reached a unanimous decision in favor of the Helpers by denying there was any legal basis for a 50 foot buffer zone, but also fined Dr. Levy's legal counsel ten thousand dollars — the greatest penalty the appellate court is permitted to impose, for knowingly and deliberately entering affidavits into the record against the Helpers that were falsely signed and falsely notarized. How far and for how long will this unjust persecution be tolerated?

I just returned last week from doing pro-life work in Europe where I found Italian officials calling for laws to restrict abortions, not encourage them. In Austria the government has just passed a law that will go into effect on January 1st, 2002 to reward a woman who has a child with two years of pay and her husband with one year of pay to encourage births rather than abortions. In Germany, to discourage abortions a woman has to seek advice from a counseling center not run by the abortionist. If she wants an abortion she is required to have a certificate showing she was counseled. Even then, she still has to wait at least seventy-two hours.

And when I returned here what did I find? A renewed attempt by the abortion industry to impost a 50 foot buffer zone on peaceful pro-lifers that would increase the number of abortions. . . . Too many young women have no knowledge of New York State's PCAP Program, namely the Prenatal Care Assistance Program. Few moms know that Gov. Pataki, in February 2000, signed into law the Baby Safe Haven Program that enables young mothers to bring their babies to a local hospital or firehouse within five days of birth without fear of prosecution for abandoning a baby. Pass this buffer law and even fewer will ever know.

Do the women take our information and act on it? You better believe they do or no new buffer zone would be called for. Every week, someone comes back to thank us. About two weeks ago . . . a woman came with a carriage with a four-months-old baby to thank me; another woman pulled up in a car with a four-year-old girl in the back seat to say thanks for being there when she needed help, and a couple stopped their car with a six-year-old boy to say thanks. This is not the result of harassment.

Since we passed the abortion law in this state in 1970, more than three million unborn children have been aborted. That is almost half the population of the city. The city's population has not increased in thirty years. That is a tragedy. The repeat rate of abortions is over fifty percent. What kind of counseling do the women receive? I meet women who are going back for their fourth, their eighth, their twelfth, their thirtieth abortion to the same abortion clinic. I know this is true because we finally reached them . . . and broke the cycle.

How can it be that a fourteen-year-old girl can go into the abortion clinic at 9 o'clock, find out she is pregnant at 10 o'clock, receive immediate temporary medicaid coverage by 10:30 and have the child in her womb terminated by 12 o'clock . . . and all this without her parents or family ever knowing. The young girl comes out at one-thirty broken, confused and weeping. The last thing young girls like that need is Intro 465 A.

Did you know that in Queens County, 64 out of
every one hundred black babies are aborted. In Kings
Country, 67 out of every 100 black babies are aborted.
That is genocide. Instead of outrage, Intro 465 A is a
proposal that will only intensify the genocide. What
is happening to our city? Over the past few years,
in the county of the Bronx, there have been more
babies aborted than born. That is a disgrace and a
shame, not a call for Intro 465 A. God knows that
the last thing this city needs is another law to make
access to abortion easier. Have we lost our minds?

About every six weeks I observe a woman who has gone
into an abortion clinic being carried out on a stretcher
to an ambulance. It happened again last Friday when
I was praying outside Ambulatory Surgery Center of
Brooklyn, and it brought back a painful memory. The
woman administrator of that clinic had called the police
and insisted they restrict me from asking a woman being
carried out on a stretcher if she was Catholic, and if so,
did she want to be anointed with the Sacrament of the
Sick. I was told this was harassment of women. Beth
Dixon, together with Dr. Levy and Francis Xavier Monck,
went to the precinct to insist that the police captain
restrain me from administering the Sacrament to the sick
and dying on a public street. The captain said, 'Msgr.
Reilly has a religious right as a priest to ask on a public
street if a person wants to receive the sacraments.' That
was not harassment. The memory of this all came back

to me last week when I saw the picture of this woman
hired by Dr. Levy and kept on the staff by Mr. Monck,
the present administrator . . . on the front pages of the
Daily News beneath the headlines 'Internet Sex Fiend,'
'Teen Held as Sex Slave.' Harassment of women indeed!

May I close my remarks by saying that if someone is
doing an injustice to me or another, then I am able to
speak to the person and address the grievance without
prior consent because of my First Amendment Rights.
In American law the exercise of First Amendment rights
are vital to bring about change without violence, to
correct wrongs within the system without revolution.
It is the concerned citizens' safety valve. No citizen
should ever lose their First Amendment rights without
clearly having done something seriously wrong that
limits their rights, and that has not been proven. To
arbitrarily pass a law that removes or limits pro-
life citizens' First Amendment rights is unfair and a
miscarriage of justice. No charges have stood the test
of strict scrutiny. All the accusations have proven to be
bogus, without foundation, or outright lies. . . . It is
unfair and unAmerican to treat citizens who are for life
as inferior. I respectfully submit that you register a 'No'
vote on Intro 465A for the sake not only of the unborn
babies whose lives will be spared, but for the sake of
sparing the mothers the grief that follows an abortion,
for the blessing and welfare of the soul of this city and
the salvation of the souls of all of us. Thank you."

It was clear when Reilly finished speaking that the Helpers had won. Kathryn Freed, the bill's sponsor, walked out of the room, Monsignor received a standing ovation, and the *Daily News* ran the full story, dealing New York abortionists one of the worst blows they'd ever received.

This was not the end of attempts on the part of the City Council to deprive the Helpers of their First Amendment rights. Neither was it the end of Monsignor's struggle to prevent ill-informed police officers from infringing on the rights of sidewalk counselors. When a clinic owner calls for help, the police have to come, and many times, the officer on duty is unaware of counselors' rights. Nevertheless, what happened on August 21, 2001, three weeks before the terrorist attack on the World Trade Center, was a signal victory for the pro-life cause and fully as important for the future of the Helpers as O'Connell's masterly defense against the Ambulatory law suit.

CHAPTER 9

THE FINAL ANALYSIS

If someone were to ask whether Monsignor's sunny phrase, "good things are happening," still applies to the work of the Helpers, the answer would be a qualified "yes." The Helpers are still marching the world over. Their counselors are still saving lives. Prayer, fasting, and public witness continue to work wonders. Fewer and fewer abortions are being performed. Clinics continue to close -- fifty-three of them in the year 2015. All to the good. But on the debit side, cardinals are no longer in the lead, publicity has fallen off (for the past several years, prayer vigils in Brooklyn and Queens haven't been covered by the diocesan newspaper), and instead of 500, 1,000 or 2500 parishioners turning out to march on a given Saturday in New York, the figure is down to 25, 30, or 35.

Things have changed in more ways than one. When Monsignor launched his apostolate, he was riding a wave of pro-life enthusiasm. Ronald Reagan had just left office after seeking to put an end to abortion, while George Bush, a kindred spirit, was newly elected. The myth of relativism had yet to sweep the country – "I'm OK, you're OK . . . my truth, your truth." Priests were still wearing the Roman collar, no one had heard the phrase "clerical sex abuse scandal," gays

were not marching in St. Patrick's Day parades, and the Supreme
Court had yet to declare gay marriage a constitutional right.

Equally to the point, the Church was led by a saint named John
Paul II, and the sees of both New York and Brooklyn were under the
aegis of men whose courage and commitment to the pro-life cause are
the stuff of legend. No one at the time could have imagined what the
second decade of the twenty-first century would bring: eight years of
presidential support for partial-birth abortion and same-sex marriage.

The miracle is that Monsignor's sunny phrase is still applicable.
Eighty-one percent of all abortion clinics that were doing business in
1991 have been shuttered. A majority of modern-day Americans, especially young Americans, describe themselves as "pro-life." During
the campaign for the Republican Party's presidential nomination in
2016, no less than three candidates, two of them Protestant, issued a
blanket condemnation of abortion, refusing even to allow an exception in cases of rape and incest.

Things today are so positive in this regard that we need to pause
for a moment and ask why. Why, in particular, have abortion rates
fallen off so dramatically? *Wrath of Angels*, one of the more informa-
tive books on the history of the pro-life movement, admits only one
reason: "a more effective and widespread use of contraception."[1] This
is the view of the so-called "qualified experts." But where is the evidence? How can one accept "improved contraceptive practice" as a
reason for abortion's decline, let alone the sole reason, when, throughout the period under review, teen pregnancy rates did not decline?[2]

The *Wrath of Angels* thesis is doubly dubious in light of the fact
that Dr. Nathanson, America's leading abortionist during the 1970s,

found that not even the abortifacient RU 486 "morning after" pill had any moderating effect on the demand for surgical abortions.[3] Another authority, Steven Mosher, who heads HLI's Population Research Institute, has demonstrated that when contraceptives are introduced, they foster an anti-life mentality and, in so doing, lead to an increase in fornication and adultery. If Mosher is right, then "improved contraception," like any other kind of contraception, merely increases the demand for abortion.

Alan Guttmacher, one-time head of Planned Parenthood, is a liberal whose opinion counts in this case because he recognized long ago that there was a growing aversion to child-killing *on moral* grounds.[4] And the facts bear him out. By 1993, 38% of abortionists admitted to moral misgivings.[5] By 1997, *Catholic New York* could report the conversion of a hundred abortion doctors.[6] In 1990, the American Bar Association and the AFL/CIO changed their position on abortion from neutral to pro-life.[7]

One can go further. In the off-year election of 1994, not a single pro-life incumbent member of Congress or governor of either party lost to a pro-choice challenger; but more than two dozen hard-core incumbent pro-choice members of Congress were defeated by pro-life challengers for a gain of forty seats in the House and six in the Senate. In the presidential election of 2016, Donald Trump, a pro-life candidate running against odds that seemed insurmountable, defeated Hillary Clinton, a radical pro-abort.

What has any of this to do with "improved contraception"?

Should we not be talking about things like crisis pregnancy centers? By offering free tests, baby supplies, and referrals for adoption counseling, they have persuaded a substantial number of moms to carry their babies to term – up to five or six women per day per center.[8]

And what of organizations such as the American Life League and Human Life International? Their mailings, along with their lobbying, have been a major factor in the decline of abortion. The only caveat is that there's still much to be done along this line. As Drollinger suggests, the average person may believe that abortion is wrong, but he doesn't see it as *terribly* wrong – as on a par, say, with first degree murder. Plenty of Catholics, aware of what the Church teaches, regard abortion as no more heinous than cheating on an exam or stealing from the rich because the leaders of the clergy are not yelling "Bloody Murder!"

It goes without saying, too, that educational institutions, important as they are, preach mainly to the choir, as compared with the Helpers, who take their stand on the street where attitudes run the gamut -- from sympathetic to indifferent to hostile. We shall return to the work of the Helpers in a moment. But first, we must allow politicians, and scientists, along with a variety of other groups, to take a bow.

Not a day goes by when the fertile imagination of a congressman doesn't invent some new means of furthering the pro-life cause. Between January of 2001 and December of 2015 approximately 288 laws were passed that tied the hands of abortionists.[9] We haven't room to list all the restrictions in all fifty states. Suffice it to say that requirements in various states include waiting periods, counseling, and examination by ultra-sound, along with parental consent for minors, higher medical standards for clinics, and prohibition of payment by Medicaid.

There are states in which a mother can be convicted of child abuse if her unborn child is harmed by alcohol, drugs, or smoking. Laws have likewise been passed that acknowledge the humanity and personhood of the unborn child. Two trips to the abortionist are sometimes required, instead of one, working a hardship on those who have to travel long distances or take days off from work and arrange for day care. In addition, the father's right to a say in the future of his unborn child has been recognized — ironically in New York, a state that allows the destruction of embryos. Texas, which has the most comprehensive pro-life laws of any state, has closed all but a few of its abortion clinics.[10]

Turning to the contribution of scientists, they have given us the fetuscope, along with DNA and the sonogram. The fetuscope, a long, optical instrument with a lens at one end and a strong light at the other, has been used to demonstrate the cruelty of late-term abortion, while the discovery of DNA has established beyond question the humanity of the child from the moment of conception. Not long ago, most folks would have said that a fetus in its early stages is "only a glob." No longer.

The sonogram, another revolutionary invention, utilizes ultrasound techniques to enable the pregnant woman to see an image of her baby. Almost always, when a mother with a baby ten weeks old or older sees an image of her child, she will keep it. Chris Slattery, the founder of Expectant Mother Care, claims that by simply parking a high tech bus in front of an abortion center in the Bronx and offering free sonograms, he has had fifteen turnarounds per week.[11] Before his conversion, Dr. Nathanson put an ultrasound machine on the abdomen of a woman undergoing an abortion and videotaped what happened: "We got a film," he says, "that was astonishing, shocking, frightening, and the pro-abortion people panicked because at that point we had moved the debate away from moralizing, sermonizing, sloganeering, and pamphleteering into a high-tech argument. For the first time, the pro-life movement had all the technology and all the smarts, and the pro-abortion people were on the defensive."

THE FEAR FACTOR

Crisis pregnancy centers, educational institutions, restrictive legislation, and science -- all played a part in furthering the cause. And then there is violence-induced fear.

Early on, we alluded to the sit-ins and bombings that preceded Reilly's founding of the Helpers in 1989. By 1991, something on the order of 40,000 pro-lifers had been arrested, and this was followed by the outright killing of abortionists.[12] In 1993, Michael Gunn, M.D. was shot dead in Pensacola, Florida, by Fundamentalist Michael Griffin. In July of the following year, Paul Hill, a Protestant minister and the father of three, killed Dr. John Britton, along with clinic escort James Barrett (despite the fact that Britton had been wearing a disguise and reclining in the back seat of his chauffeur-driven car on his way to work).[13] During the last week of December, 1994, John Salvi III, a mentally disturbed Catholic, killed two clinic workers and wounded five others in Brookline, Massachusetts. Four years later, James Kopp, a devout Catholic and convert, killed an abortionist doctor by the name of Barnett Slepian in his Amherst home near Buffalo. Slepian's replacement, brought in from out of town, had to be escorted to his workplace by federal marshals.

Clearly, terror was in the air, and there were consequences. One woman, traumatized by the violence, decided against having an abortion.[14] A facility in New York's Nassau County closed as a result of Salvi's gunfire in Massachusetts.[15] Insurance rates soared for clinics and hospitals doing abortions. Security cameras and bullet-proof glass had to be installed, additional escorts and guards had to be hired, and none of this was cheap.[16] There were abortionists who dared not walk in front of their windows at night without drawing the drapes.[17] Some took to wearing body armor that covered their chest, pelvic area, and upper legs, while others varied their route to work. Homes were picketed. "WANTED" signs with a picture of the abortionist were posted all over town.

This said, the impact of violence, even low-level violence, was not necessarily what one expected. Sit-ins, for example, saved only four or five babies per week in the relatively favorable climate of St. Louis.[18] Clients who are turned away from a clinic on Monday can return on Tuesday. During the initial period of civil disobedience, the abortion rate *kept rising* and didn't begin to fall until Monsignor Reilly's Helpers came into the picture.

In 1978, pro-lifers occupied an abortion clinic in Manchester, Missouri, run by Dr. Bolivar Escobedo. Joan Andrews broke her finger at this site while wrestling with the police, and the initial results of the sit-in appeared promising. Clients were discouraged from coming and Escobedo seemed to be on the verge of bankruptcy. Ultimately, though, he obtained a court order that put an end to the protest, and not only did he continue to practice. He opened two more mills and, as a self-proclaimed Catholic with children in Catholic schools, he got Archbishop John May of St. Louis to take sides against the rescuers.[19]

Few would deny that sit-ins saved lives, but they also inflamed public opinion to such an extent that Congress enacted back-breaking legislation in 1994 -- the Freedom of Access to Clinic Entrances (FACE) -- mentioned earlier. By driving up the cost of fines and lengthening jail terms to the point where civil disobedience was impracticable, FACE effectively shut down Operation Rescue.

Another problem with violence, even of the non-violent kind, is that it tends to escalate into actions like kidnapping, firebombing, and murder, with results that are again mixed. Four years after the Escobedo incident, Illinois child-killer Hector Zevallos was kidnapped by members of the radical Army of God. But after being held for eight days and released, he went back to his clinic to do more abortions.

In 1986, a Wichita clinic belonging to Dr. George Tiller was firebombed, but Tiller carried on. In 1991, the entrance to his clinic was blocked by Operation Rescue during what Terry called the "Summer of Mercy" -- 2600 were arrested for civil disobedience at three different clinics in Wichita, with Tiller's mill the principal target. But once again, he carried on. Two years later, he was shot him in both arms. And the upshot? He went right on with his business. Even after he was gunned down in 2009, a woman who admired his courage during the Summer of Mercy bought his property and found doctors willing to continue the practice. MDs were flown in and picked up at undisclosed airports by drivers who advised them to lie down and stay out of sight. The woman herself, after learning how to identify bombs under her car, began wearing a bullet-proof vest, and to this day, Tiller's clinic remains open.[20]

One of the greatest drawbacks of violence of any sort is that it splits the pro-life movement while acting as a deterrent to peaceful protest. The following is an eyewitness description of the effect of clinic bombings in Florida in 1984: "It's like people were spooked. They didn't want to do anything. No picketing, no sidewalk counseling. People were afraid if they even wrote a letter to the editor against abortion, their neighbors would say, 'Are you one of those bombers?'"[21]

In 1984, at a rescue in Wheaton, Maryland, forty-seven rescuers were arrested, including seventeen clergy. The event captured the attention of the media. But two days later, the site was bombed, and the moment this happened, support from the clergy evaporated.[22] It was the same with the Salvi killings in Brookline where the Helpers were active. Cardinal Law of Boston not only advised his people to boycott the Helpers' prayer vigils; he forbade his priests from celebrating their Masses.

Although Bishop Daily of Brooklyn reacted to the Brookline killings by praying at additional sites, Monsignor found himself hard-pressed to counter charges that his work was incendiary.[23] He had to assure reporters that his people were non-confrontational, that none of them had ever been arrested. "We are conscientious objectors, not revolutionists," he told the press:

> Once we resort to force, we have become the judge, the
> jury, and the enforcer. We are a threat to society. The
> Founding Fathers foresaw the kind of injustice and
> dissension that would engender opposition, even hate,
> and they didn't want civil war over it. So they passed
> the First Amendment to the Constitution, a built-in
> safety valve giving people who disagree with the law the
> right to assemble, protest, demonstrate, and, in the case
> of the Helpers, do sidewalk counseling. It is enough
> to make the truth known. The rest we leave to God.

What would happen, he asked, if there wasn't a peaceful, prayerful way for pro-life Americans to work off their frustration and anger over the holocaust? Would they not find another outlet? Needless to say, he made it equally clear that his abhorrence of the Salvi killings was no greater than his abhorrence of what the victims of such violence had done to thousands of innocent children:

> I find their pleas and demands for the condemnation
> of the killing of the abortionist . . . to be shallow and
> inconsistent because of their silence, even approval,
> of the slaughter of the innocent unborn by the same
> abortionist. It is common sense that the Law of God,
> Thou Shalt Not Kill applies to all human beings without
> exception . . . . The Helpers strongly condemn both the
> actions of Dr. John Britton [the abortionist] and Paul

Hill [Britton's killer] and so should our government and Supreme Court. To condemn one and not the other is insane and leaves the door open to further insanity.

THE HELPERS' CONTRIBUTION

In sum, sit-ins were politically indefensible in the long run, but by sensitizing Americans to the evil in their midst, they raised the level of national consciousness and, in so doing, acted as a stepping stone to the kind of peaceful, non-confrontational activity introduced by Monsignor Reilly.

Which brings us, full circle, to the Helpers' contribution. Had their founder done nothing more than take the wind out of the sails of right-wing extremists whose resort to violence threatened to derail the pro-life movement, his initiative would have been golden. But his contribution goes a great deal further. By furnishing a peaceful mode of expression for anti-abortion protest, he made it possible for the average person to defend the innocent without fear of being arrested or sued. Helpers don't have to carve out large chunks of time from a busy schedule, which is another advantage. An hour or two on the street once a month will do. Workers, non-workers, children, grandparents, students, clergy – all can participate.

Key to their success, as we have seen, is the element of sacrifice, and this is something that bears repeating. History testifies to the fact that prayer and fasting have worked wonders, especially when combined with risk-taking. Tertullian, one of the ancient Church Fathers, remarked famously that "the blood of martyrs is the seed of the Church." The Helpers may not have shed blood the way Peter and Paul did, but when they leave the comfort of their living room to go public, they expose themselves to insult, as well as inclement weather. Some return home exhausted.

Etched indelibly on my memory is the image of Monsignor leading a Helpers prayer vigil as he approached his eighty-second birthday. In declining health, he shuffled his way to a killing site. The mercury stood at five degrees below zero, and the wind was strong. I offered him hand warmers, but he wouldn't take them. He wouldn't even wear gloves. By the time we reached the abortion clinic, he was no longer shuffling; he was tottering. Yet the only concession he would make to the bitter cold was to say one less rosary. On his return to church, he needed assistance to make the last block. Then, when he reached the sacristy to prepare for Benediction and was urged to sit down for a moment to catch his breath, the answer was "no." Absolutely not!

It's a good thing that he is a man of faith because physical infirmity is the least of his problems. Almost all of his close friends have either passed away or fallen by the wayside. Over the years, he has seen his countrymen plunge ever deeper into the mire of immorality. Meanwhile, the Church that he loves has shrunk, all too often, from heroic confrontation with evil. Well might he echo Elijah's lament at the foot of Mt. Horeb: "I alone am left."

IN THE FINAL ANALYSIS

Monsignor's life has been one long Lent – albeit Lent with a smile. Someone once offered to buy him a new car to replace his twenty-seven-year-old rattle trap, and, of course, he wouldn't hear of it. I can still see the gleam in his eye!

He has been called the "Pro-life Superman" and honored many times over for his dedication, organizational ability, and skill as a public speaker. In 2015, at the age of 81, he gave an introductory talk, as well as the closing address, for the World Congress for Life at Fatima. Additional marks of recognition include the Cardinal Cooke Right-to-Life Award, along with the Legatus International Cardinal O'Connor Pro-Life Award; the United States Conference of Catholic Bishops People of Life Award; and the Human Life International Cardinal Von Galen Pro-Life Award.

Oskar Schindler saved over a thousand Jews from almost certain extinction during World War II, and his story was told in a popular movie, *Schindler's List*. Raoul Wallenberg, for saving tens of thousands, was awarded the U.S. Congressional Gold Medal and commemorated on U.S. postage stamps though he was not an American. Why not the Nobel Prize for Monsignor? He has saved *scores of thousands* and brought peace of mind to at least as many parents by serving, both in season and out of season, as a sidewalk counselor. In addition, he has led prayer vigils around the world and trained untold numbers of Helpers in the most successful method of sidewalk counseling ever devised. John Paul the Great warned that "there can be no peace when this most basic good [human life] is not protected" while Mother Teresa of Calcutta, herself a Nobel laureate, went even further, calling abortion the greatest threat to peace.[1]

Mother Teresa and Monsignor have much in common. Her Missionaries of Charity offer the tenderest of love to souls who have been abandoned, and is this not what the Helpers do for little ones yet to be born, recognizing them as brothers and sisters, welcoming them into the human family, embracing them spiritually, and standing with them when they die? The Missionaries are often depicted as mere social workers when, in fact, they are a lot more. They see Jesus in the face of the outcast and regard themselves as doing acts of kindness to their Lord. Likewise, in the case of the Helpers. Whereas the secular world regards them as mere protestors bent on saving babies' lives, they see themselves standing with Mary and John at the foot of the Cross.

Both Mother Teresa and Monsignor Reilly were high school principals who exchanged a life of honor and security for one of dishonor and insecurity. She pictured herself as "only a little wire; God is the power." He, for his part, tells his Helpers, "We are [only] the stones He uses – our poverty and nothingness."

In risking their lives for the sake of the defenseless, both Mother and Monsignor died to self in a culture that frowned upon them. Teresa, ridiculed for taking to the street, was treated as a pariah, even by her religious order. Reilly, disdained for taking to the street, has encountered indifference from many of the Church's pastors.

The long and short of it is that Mother Teresa and Monsignor Reilly came unto their own, and their own received them not, the only difference being that one of them is a Nobel laureate, while the other remains a no-namer. Ask almost any Catholic if they've heard of Monsignor Reilly, and almost always, the answer is "no" because his fellow priests have done little to publicize his work: "A prophet is not without honor except in his own country, among his own kindred, and in his own house."[2]

Monsignor, who uses the phrase "no-namer" to describe his Helpers -- "ordinary people doing ordinary things to get extraordinary results" – knows that the Church's roster of saints is loaded with no-namers. One thinks of Thérèse of Lisieux, Solanus Casey, Pier Georgio Frassati, and André Bessette. During their lifetime, few, if any, of these great-hearted individuals were recognized by anyone outside their immediate circle of family and friends. So, too, with the Helpers. Their work is thankless, their standing in the eyes of the Almighty a well-kept secret, because they are content to do everything for the glory of God. As for their founder and executive director, he has been loyal to his priestly duties and unwavering in defense of the truth, which reminds me of something he himself once said of the late Terence Cardinal Cooke: "There is nothing stronger than a real gentleman. He was unchangeable and uncompromising."

POSTSCRIPT

I urge those who are moved to stand at Calvary in a special act of love for God's precious infants to contact the Helpers. A team leader in their neighborhood will reach out to them, and if any of them wishes to be a sidewalk counselor, they will receive training. In the words of Joan Andrews:

> Maybe you'll be able directly to save some lives, maybe not. What's even more important, you'll be there. In a sense, it may be a way to redeem the abandonment of Jesus by His apostles when they refused to be with Him at His death – too often, we also refuse to be with Jesus for fear of the Cross, do we not? These little ones dying today are intricately connected with the sufferings and death of Our Savior. There is a bond here that must not be overlooked. All the political action, educating, donation of funds, demonstrations, alternative work, important and necessary as these are, do not make up for an absence at the death scene. Thus, let me beg you to view your presence at the killing center in your area as the place where God wants you to be. Grab your Rosary, pick up your Bible, bring your devotionals, and go out to the Calvary not far from you – where Christ is being crucified today in your midst. We may not be able to save their

lives, but can we not plead on their behalf? And should
they die, as usually happens (God forgive us!), let us lift
up our hearts to God Almighty on their behalf . . . It will
be the only human love they will know on this earth.

END NOTES

PROLOGUE

[1] *New York Times*, 6/16/94.

CHAPTER 1

[1] Mal. 2:16.

[2] Matt. 5:27-32.

[3] Matt. 4:10.

[4] Frederick W. Marks, *A Brief for Belief*, 54.

[5] John 8:32.

[6] Wikopedia (entry on Nathanson).

[7] Meaghan Winter, "The Stealth Attack on Abortion," *New York Times*, 11/12/15, A35.

[8] Helpers of God's Precious Infants News Letter (hereafter HNL), 3/17/97.

[9] Robert Cetrulo, *Reflections of a Pro-life Warrior*, 12.

[10] Quoted by Cetrulo in *Reflections*, 13.

[11] Siegfried Ernst, *Man the Greatest of Miracles*, 79, 108.

[12] *The Tablet*, 11/23/02.

[13] Ernst, *Man the Greatest of Miracles*, 132.

[14] Joseph Scheidler, *Closed: 99 Ways to Stop Abortion*, 299.

CHAPTER 2

[1] Bernard Nathanson, *The Hand of God*, 128, 187, 191-93.

CHAPTER 3

[1] Risen and Thomas, *Wrath of Angels*, 74.

[2] *Ibid.*, 74, 200.

[3] *The Tablet* of the Brooklyn diocese (hereafter simply *The Tablet*) quoting the *New York Times* 5/31/03.

[4] HNL, 1/1/09, p. 1.

[5] *New York Post*, 2/21/90.

[6] *The Wanderer*, 2/6/92.

[7] HNL 1/1/09, p. 1.

[8] *Evangelium Vitae*, Section 25.

CHAPTER 4

[1] *The Wanderer*, 2/6/92.

[2] HNL, 10/21/96.

[3] HNL, 12/20/91.

[4] HNL, 12/28/96.

[5] *Catholic Twin Circle*, 5/17/90, p. 7.

[6] *Bay Ridge Courier*, 8/26/91.

[7] Mary Arnold, "One Woman's Journey" (interview with a former abortion escort) in *Catholic Twin Circle*, 2/9/92.

[8] HNL, Summer 2003.

[9] *New York Times*, 3/31/93; 2/20/95 (pp. A1, B2); 10/29/98. Rickie Solinger, *Abortion Wars*, 248.

[10] *New York Times*, 6/16/94.

[11] Faye Ginsberg, "Rescuing the Nation" in Solinger, ed., *Abortion Wars*, 227.

[12] Anna Quindlen, "Public and Private: Beyond Doctors," *New York Times*, 4/21/93, A23.

[13] Hebrews 9:22.

[14] *The Tablet*, 11/10/90.

[15] For the pail of water, see *The Tablet*, 1/27/07; on Doris Rosa, see John Burger, "Non-Violent Witness," *Catholic New York*, 8/5/93, p. 17.

[16] For the shoving incident, see *New York Daily News*, 8/12/90.

[17] *The Tablet*, 5/31/03.

[18] Margaret Driscoll and Emily Faugno, *Saving Women and Infants from Abortion*, 33, 56.

[19] 1 Col. 1:24 (quoted in HNL, 10/7/00).

[20] HNL, 1998; Reilly Address to the World Congress for Life, October 2010 ("For Twenty-one Years the Helpers Have Been Under the Protection of the Virgin Mary"), *World Congress Compendium*, p. 106 -- a compendium of Monsignor Reilly's Speeches (first edition).

[21] HNL, Lent 2003.

[22] Bill Donohue, *The Catholic Advantage*, 107.

CHAPTER 5

[1] *The Tablet*, 6/20/92; *New York Daily News* (10/1/12), p. 32.

[2] *New York Guardian*, May 1992, p. 5. According to *The Tablet*, the number of marchers was 2,000 (6/29/92). Monsignor's figure is 5,000.

[3] *Catholic New York*, 6/18/92, p. 3.

[4] *New York Times*, 6/14/92, p. 2.

[5] *Ibid.*

[6] Maria Newman, "O'Connor Leads March on Abortion," *New York Times*, 6/14/92, p. 2.

[7] *Catholic New York*, 6/18/92, p. 3.

CHAPTER 6

[1] HNL, Summer 2003.

[2] HNL, Fall 2005, p. 2; *Compendium*, 115-16.

[3] HNL, Fall 2005, p. 1.

[4] HNL, Fall 2005, p. 6.

[5] Scheidler, "The Power of Prayer on the Abortion Front," *Fatima Crusader* (Winter 1998), pp. 41-43.

CHAPTER 7

[1] HNL 8/20/09, p. 8.

[2] HNL 8/6/04, p. 3.

[3] HNL 1/31/02.

[4] HNL, 5/1/02; HNL, 8/20/08, p. 1; HNL, 9/4/02.

[5] *Homiletic and Pastoral Review* (April 1999), p. 80.

[6] HNL, April 12, 2006.

[7] HNL, 4/2/06, p. 1.

[8] HNL, Lent 2003.

[9] HNL, 10/1/06, p. 1

[10] For the Al-Qaeda comparison, see *The Tablet*, 8/31/02.

[11] Fred Kaplan, *John Quincy Adams: American Visionary*, 462.

[12] Philip J. Reilly, *World Congress Compendium* (first edition), 121-22.

[13] *Ibid.*, 118.

[14] HNL, January 2005.

[15] HNL, 11/1/06.

[16] HNL, 8/10/09, p. 8; HNL, 8/28/99, p. 4.

[17] Philip J. Reilly to the Speaker of the New York State Assembly, April 2, 1970.

[18] E. g. HNL, January 2005, p. 1.

CHAPTER 8

[1] Diane Cardwell, "Debate Flares Over Proposal for Buffer Zones at Clinics," *New York Times*, 8/22/01, B3.

[2] *Ibid.*

[3] *New York Daily News*, 8/22/01, p. 3.

[4] *New York Daily News*, 8/15/01, pp. 2-3; *New York Times*, 8/14/01, B1.

CHAPTER 9

[1] Risen and Thomas, *Wrath of Angels*, 376.

[2] *USA Today*, 6/16/94, p. 1.

[3] Nathanson, *Hand of God*, 98-99,

[4] *USA Today*, 6/16/94, p. 1.

[5] *New York Daily News*, 8/12/90.

[6] *Project Choice Report*, February 1993.

[7] *Catholic New York*, 11/20/97.

[8] *The Wanderer*, 11/1/90, p. 7.

[9] *New York Times*, 12/20/15, p. A10.

[10] *Ibid.*

[11] *The Tablet*, 11/29/08, p. 3.

[12] Daniel K. Williams, *Defenders of the Unborn*, 263.

[13] Faye Ginsberg, "Rescuing the Nation," in Solinger, ed., *Abortion Wars*, 227.

[14] *New York Daily News*, 9/2/98.

[15] *New York Times*, 11/7/98, p. B4.

[16] Risen and Thomas, *Wrath of Angels*, 200.

[17] *Ibid.*

[18] Andrews, *I Will Never Forget You*, 56.

[19] *Ibid.*, 44-56.

[20] *Los Angeles Times*, 3/27/13, p. A7.

[21] *You Reject Them, You Reject Me: The Prison Letters of Joan Andrews*, 83.

[22] *New York Times*, 11/4/98, D8.

[23] *The Tablet*, 1/28/95.

CONCLUSION

[1] John Paul was quoted in HNL 1/6/01.

[2] Mark 6:4.

APPENDICES

APPENDIX A:

MONSIGNOR'S DESCRIPTION OF THE HELPERS' MISSION

The Helpers of God's Precious Infants is a group of people committed to maintaining a loving and prayerful presence outside the abortion mills where God's children are put to death. We unite ourselves with these victims in solidarity with their pain as they are put to death at this modern-day Calvary. We pray in reparation for the injustice . . . . Just as Mary and John lovingly stood and prayed beneath Jesus' Cross as He died, we wish to remain with these children in the hour that they are crucified.

We pray to obtain God's mercy for the abortionist and his staff who do the killing. Our peaceful presence outside their mill is a reproach to the dirty business they carry on inside. Some abortionists have stopped doing abortions because of the pressure from groups picketing outside their offices. Our prayerful witness outside the death center where he works tells the abortionist and his neighbors that we refuse to recognize or accept abortion as an appropriate or legitimate profession. The consciences of the abortion mill staff will be disturbed by our presence there, making them feel ashamed so that they can reform their lives and switch to a suitable line of work, one that will contribute to society, not destroy it. Regular people in normal jobs don't want to have to pass by a crowd of people praying every time they go to their office. The workers at the abortion mill should feel uncomfortable when they come to work. It should not be pleasant to get up in the morning to come to destroy children. They should have to confront God each time they start their day of business, because it is His precious children they are attacking. The message of the Helpers of God's Precious Infants to the abortionist is that, though we love them, we will *never* accept what they do.

We *witness* to those who pass by, praying that they will take notice of what is going on and be moved to take action against the killing in their neighborhood. Many neighbors and businesses that surround the killing center don't like having babies die right near where they live and work, but they have resigned themselves to the fact that the evil is there and assume it can't be eliminated. When they see that something can be done, that it is not necessary to tolerate this death camp in their midst, they will join us. We help the community to see that they, also, are responsible for the deaths of these children, so close to where they live. They permit the evil to continue by their failure to rise up against it.

We *plead* with our voices for the lives of the babies being carried in by the pregnant women who have scheduled appointments with the abortionist that day. We ask each mother to change her mind. We reach out to her with the love of Christ; we do not judge or condemn her for what she is planning to do. We simply promise *support* and *assistance* if she should change her mind, and prayers for her healing and conversion if she should proceed with the killing of her child.

Most of all, we *love* the unborn children who will be brought there that day. These children have been rejected by their parents and are doomed to die. The only human love they may ever encounter in their short lives may be from those of us standing outside.

No one wants to be alone when they die. When our loved ones lie at death's door in intensive care units, we keep constant watch. Many prayers are said outside of the dying person's room. Even Jesus did not want to be alone before He died. He asked His apostles to watch with Him in prayer through the night. Our loving presence for the children at their hour of death will comfort the Heart of God, because they belong to Him.

Helpers come to the abortion mill for an hour or more on a morning when babies are scheduled to be killed and they wage an extremely important spiritual battle. They pray in a spirit of reparation for their own sins, for the sin of abortion, and for the well being of the babies whose lives weigh in the balance. They pray, above all, for women bent on killing their children, but also for the abortionist and his staff, along with the neighboring community. Finally, they pray for the legislators, for the religious leaders of the nation, and for all who, through indifference, do nothing to put abortion on the road to extinction.

Those who come to provide spiritual and moral support for the sidewalk counselors are essential. Before a mother is able to physically abort her child, a "spiritual abortion" takes place within her heart. By the time she arrives at the abortion mill, she has already rejected her child. This "spiritual abortion" must be overcome by spiritual means before the mother can change her mind about the physical abortion. Through sacrifice and prayers, the Helpers obtain the grace of God that is needed to reverse the "spiritual abortion."

Those who come to pray are also there to give their personal love to God's infants who will die that day. Just as John the Baptist leapt for joy in Elizabeth's womb because he was aware of the presence of the love of Jesus and Mary (remember that it was at the sound of Mary's voice that he leapt in his mother's womb), so also will the babies leap for joy in their mother's womb when they hear the voices of the Helpers because they will know they are loved.

It is against a backdrop of prayer, therefore, that the Helpers counsel the woman going in to have the abortion and ask her to reconsider her decision. Oftentimes, it is found that the woman going for an abortion has not been given much factual information about what is about to happen. The Helpers' counselors educate her about the baby's biological development in her womb, and help her to understand the exact manner in which the abortion will kill her child. They will also warn her of the physical harm the abortion may cause to her own body. The woman will, at the same time, be provided with literature telling of all the help available, financial, medical, and spiritual. Finally, the counselors will talk to the father of the baby. And if the woman decides to see the abortionist anyway, she will be reminded that the Helpers are not going to stop praying for her and her child, that they will remain outside the mill waiting to see if she, like others before her, changes her mind and comes back out again with her baby intact. It does happen. I know of the case of a woman who, at the last second, pulled the anesthesia needle out of her arm, got up from the abortionists' operating table, and left the doctor and the staff standing there in shock.

If the woman comes back out, having rejected counsel and undergone an abortion, she is still in serious need of help if the guilt from her abortion is not to weigh so heavily that it leads to still another abortion, and then another. As Margaret Driscoll and Emily Faugno put it in their memoir, subtitled *A Dance in the Rain*, abortion is an unnatural act. When a woman has an abortion, she puts a wall up around her heart. She becomes desensitized as a way of surviving and avoiding the tears.

APPENDIX B:

THE HELPERS HANDOUT – SPECIFICS

Under the heading, "Abortion – Possible Health Risks" readers are warned of unpleasant possibilities such as perforation of the uterus or cervix, increased likelihood of cervical cancer, death, retained placenta of fetal parts, and complications for future pregnancies. Mental risks are listed as well. They include feelings of guilt and anxiety; suicidal thoughts; sexual dysfunction; eating disorders; drug and alcohol abuse; repeat abortions.

Under the heading of "Abortion Pill," women learn that they may have to agree to have a surgical abortion if the pill doesn't work; also that health risks of the pill include heavy bleeding/hemorrhaging; infection; death; vomiting; diarrhea, severe pain; and damage to the uterus. Readers are invited to visit www.abortionpillrisks.com for more information.

"Possible Health Risks of Contraceptives" are listed as blood clots which can cause strokes; breast cancer; cervical cancer; infertility; weight gain; mental depression; and abortifacient results. Those who desire additional information are referred to www.thepillkills.org.

Pictures of babies at various stages of fetal development are featured in order to reveal their amazingly high level of development at the age of ten weeks. And for reasons mentioned earlier, the handout concludes with a list of organizations that have post-abortion healing programs:

Lumina -- http//postabortionhelporg/pah (877-586-4621) or email lumina@postabortionhelp.org.

Sisters of Life 866-575-0075 hopeandhealing@sistersoflife.org

Rachel's Helpers 718-939-6646

A Lamp for Life

APPENDIX C:

AUTHOR'S LETTER TO THE NOBEL
PEACE PRIZE COMMITTEE

APRIL 7, 2017

Nobel Prize Committee
Stortinget
P. O. Box 1700 Sentum
N-0026
Oslo, Norway

To the Committee:

I should like to nominate Monsignor Philip J. Reilly for the Nobel Peace Prize. Almost single-handedly, he has reclaimed the American pro-life movement from a course of violence and redirected it to a campaign of peaceful witness to the sacredness of human life. Where once we had bombings, killings, and civil disobedience, we now have police-protected prayer vigils for conversion, mercy, and healing.

Over the past twenty-seven years, Monsignor Reilly has not only saved an estimated 100,000 lives of unborn children. He has (a) brought peace to the hearts of at least as many parents, (b) trained hundreds in his method of non-confrontational street counseling, and (c) established chapters of his organization (the Helpers of God's Precious Infants) in all major US cities, along with thirty countries overseas. If, as Mother Teresa of Calcutta (herself a Nobel laureate) believed, abortion is the greatest cause of discord, strife, and turmoil in our world, then Reilly is beyond compare as a champion of peace.

I would be happy to send you a well-documented manuscript of 150 pages describing the work of this remarkable individual — a story that has never been told. Let me know if it would be helpful to you in your deliberations.

I look forward to hearing from you.

Sincerely,

Frederick W. Marks, Ph.D.

KEY DATES

1930   Lambeth Conference of Anglicans approves artificial contraception.

1959   The Pill is introduced in the US.

1960   Monsignor Reilly's ordination.

The Pill, still illegal, is distributed as a medical solution for irregular menstrual cycles.

1965   *Griswold v. Connecticut* legalizes the Pill for married couples.

10/4, at the UN, Paul VI defends the sacredness of human life and condemns artificial birth control.

1967   Abortion is legalized in the UK.

Colorado becomes the first state to legalize abortion in the US.

Bishops launch the National Right to Life Committee, soon to be independent of the hierarchy.

1967-70   Reilly's bus trips to Albany to lobby, as well as street demonstrations to stop legalization.

1967-89   Reilly is actively involved in every aspect of the pro-life movement.

1968   July 25 – *Humanae Vitae* reiterates the Church's condemnation of contraception and requires "grave" reasons for Natural Family Planning (Sections #10 and 17).

California legalizes abortion with Reagan signature (RR later converted by Mildred Jefferson).

1970   NY legalizes abortion up to 6 months.

1970-72

Street demonstrations and lobbying.

Ultrasound becomes available circa 1972.

1972   Abortion legalization is repealed in NY, but the repeal is vetoed by Governor Rockefeller.

1973   January 22: *Roe v. Wade* and *Doe v. Bolton* legalize abortion nationwide practically through 9 months.

1974   First March for Life in Washington, D.C.

1973-83

Cardinal Cooke, chairman of the bishops' committee for pro-life activities, declares October Respect for Life month.

1975   August 2 – Sit-in in Rockville, MD may be the nation's first (*Wrath of Angels*, 62).

1976   March – first documented act of violence (setting fire to Planned Parenthood facility in Eugene, Oregon by Joseph Stockett – see *Wrath of Angels*, 74).

September 30 -- Hyde Amendment is approved but suspended after 4 hrs. by injunction (not upheld until 1980 by Supreme Court).

1977   Sit-ins in St. Louis Jan. 18 (at Escobedo Clinic).

Rescuers set fire to Planned Parenthood facility in St. Paul, MN (*Wrath of Angels*, 74).

1978   Sit-in at NYC clinic founded by Bernard Nathanson helps move Nathanson away from abortion.

Reilly participates in Death Valley walk of 100 miles.

1979   Founding of American Life League (ALL) by Judie Brown.

1979-84

JP II theology of the body talks for general catechetical audiences.

1980   Joe Scheidler founds the Pro-Life Action League.

1980-81

Fr. Marx founds Human Life International with the aid of Judie Brown.

The constitutionality of the Hyde Amendment is upheld by the Supreme Court.

1980s   First prayer at abortion mills.

1982   Kidnapping of Illinois abortionist Hector Zevallo by the Army of God, which earlier fire-bombed Florida clinics.

1984   Cardinal O'Connor defends civil disobedience when his auxiliary bishop, Emerson Moore, is arrested for protesting apartheid in front of the South African consulate in NYC.

Pensacola, Florida mills bombed late in the year by born-again Christians, driving up the cost of insurance.

By 1984, John Cavanaugh-O'Keefe, the father of rescue, is trying to get Protestants involved (*Wrath of Angels*, 77).

1985   First showing of *Silent Scream*.

Army of God plants bombs at clinics in MD, VA, and D.C.

1986   Randall Terry founds Operation Rescue and, for the first
            time, is arrested.
            Pensacola sit-in March 26.
            Joan Andrews begins Florida jail term April 23.
            Dr. Tiller's clinic in Wichita is firebombed.

1987   Randall Terry becomes prominent for blockading clinics.
            The CFRs are founded (Franciscans Friars of the Renewal).
            November – first Operation Rescue outside Philadelphia
                at the Cherry Hill Women's Center. One account
                says 210 arrested, another 400.
            December 3: Fr. James Lisante of Rockville Center backs
                Operation Rescue. He is the highest Church official
                to do so, and on December 28, he brings out 2 bish-
                ops, 150-200 priests, and 4000 people to picket a
                local abortion clinic.
            Meanwhile, on December 26, Joan Andrews is released
                from solitary confinement (though she is still in jail).

1987-89
            Bishop Daily leads Palm Beach prayer vigils.

1988   Huge Rescue during Dem. Nat. Conv. at Atlanta. Police
            turn brutal.
            May 1988 to September 1989, Msgr. Reilly is involved in
            Rescue.
            Huge New York Rescue operation May 2-5 with Vaughan
            and Bavaro (503 arrests) nudges Nathanson toward be-
            lief in God; 500 arrested in protest at gynecologist office
            (E. 85th St., NYC).
            Mid-year, Joan Andrews is finally released from prison.

1989   Helpers of God's Precious Infants is founded Oct. 7.

1990   Bishop Daily comes to Brooklyn (named to the post in Feb.).

Terry steps down as head of Operation Rescue.

June – 1st large Helpers prayer vigil – to Choices with Daily on Queens Blvd. 1,000 marchers; 150 police officers.

1991   Huge six-week Rescue in Wichita ("Summer of Mercy) with" 1600-2600 arrests.

Monsignor leaves Cathedral Prep in June to become chaplain at Precious Blood Monastery.

The Sisters of Life are founded.

Burning of abortionist's home and barn, along with 20 horses, in Bellevue, Nebraska by the Lambs of Christ.

Number of abortions begins long-term decline.

1992   Early in 1992, Cardinal Mahony of Los Angeles leads 1100 in Helpers vigil.

Huge Rescue in Buffalo (1000 protesters and 500 arrests).

But all four of Buffalo's abortion mills remain open.

Fr. Pavone takes over Priests for Life.

June 13: Cardinal O'Connor leads huge prayer vigil in NYC.

1993   Jan. *Bray v. Alexandria* Supreme Court decision 6-3 (upholds sidewalk counselors' rights against Ku Klux Klan act).

Killing of Dr. Gunn in March by Fundamentalist Michael Griffin in Pensacola.

Non-fatal shooting of Dr. Tiller in August by Shelley Shannon (Army of God) wounding him in both arms.

1994   Clinton signs Freedom of Access to Clinic Entrances (FACE) bill into law May 26.

St. Patrick's desecrated by gays.

NYC Clinic Access Law enacted, making it a crime to block or obstruct patients or staff.

Madsen v. Women's Health Center upholds rights of sidewalk counselors – no arbitrary buffer zones.

Killing of Dr. Britton and escort James Barrett in July by Paul Hill, a Protestant minister with three children, in Pensacola. Cardinal Bevilacqua leads 1200 Oct. 15 in prayer vigil.

Killing of 2 workers and wounding of five others Dec. 30 by Catholic John Salvi in Brookline, MA.

Cardinal Law shuts down the Boston Helpers after the violence.

1997   Ambulatory Surgery Center lawsuit filed against Helpers.

Schenck v. Pro-Life Network upholds counselors' rights.

Army of God bombings in Atlanta and Birmingham.

1998   Oct. 23 –**Killing** of abortionist Barnett Slepian by Catholic convert James Kopp near Buffalo (Kopp a Lamb of Christ).

2001   August 21 – NYC Council of Public Safety Committee meeting on frozen zone "gag rule" (just three weeks before 9/11). White powder mailings to abortionists by Army of God.

2003   Congress bans partial-birth abortion.

2007   *Gonzales v. Carhart* -- all 5 Catholic justices on Supreme Ct. uphold a Nebraska ban of partial-birth abortion, as well as a the congressional ban of 2003.

2008   Helpers fight against NYC Council bill INTRO 826, which is offered as an amendment to a 1994 bill.

2009   May – protests at Notre Dame by Lambs' Fr. Weslin (re: Obama as commencement speaker). Many arrests.

    May 31: **Killing of late-term abortionist George Tiller** in his church by Scott Roeder.

    Sept. **Murder** of pro-life "sign guy" James Pouillon in Owosso, MI by James Harlan Drake.

    Late 2009: Lambs' Weslin sit-in at House Speaker Pelosi's office, shredding of 4,000-page copies of Obamacare, strewn over floor, with Weslin lying down on office threshold, waiting to be carried away by police.

    Brooklyn's diocesan newspaper, *The Tablet*, ceases to cover Reilly's prayer vigils.

2015   **Killing** on Nov. 27 by Robert Dear of three and wounding of nine at Planned Parenthood clinic in Colorado Springs. Dear was a self-described anti-abortion "warrior." This caused a hospital in the state of Washington to tell abortion doctors not to accept requests for interviews or articles as a matter of prudence (NYT, 5/3/16, A10).

INDEX

Abortion, ix, xii

backup for contraception, 3, 12

decline of, 39, 46-47, 135-39

effect on blacks, 4

fatal for mothers, 69 (one instance)

health risks, 167

lies told by pro-aborts, 5-7

pro-abort tactics (see pro-choice
tactics)

profit from, 167

state-wide legal restrictions, 138-39

Supreme Court rulings, 5, 11, 21,
23, 47, 126, 173, 175-76

Abruzzino, Rosemary, vii, 20, 34

Adams, John Quincy, 107

Adasevic, Stojan, 87-88

Agency for International Development,
93

Ambulatory Surgery Center, 61-63,
119-24, 132, 134, 176

American Civil Liberties Union, 43,
126

American Life League, 10, 13, 138

Andrews, Joan, 11-12, 27, 141, 151,
174

Angelica.

See Mother Angelica

Arinze, Francis Cardinal, 94

Army of God, 173, 175-76

Austria, 88-89, 130

Barrett, James, 140, 176

Benedict XVI, 94

Bereit, David, 86

Bevilacqua, Anthony Cardinal, 176

Birth control.

See Contraception

Bishops.

See National Conference of
Catholic Bishops

Blackmun, Harry, 118

Blacks, 17, 91

Bray v. Alexandria, 175

Bright Dawn Ministry, 13

Britton, MD, John, 140, 144-45,
176

Brown, Judie, 10-12

Bruno, Rev. Michael, vii

Buckley, James, 25

Cano, Sandra, 6

Carroll, Warren, 2

Cathedral Prep, 16, 20, 32, 40, 78,
        103, 175

Center for Reproductive and Sexual
        Health, 25

Cherry Hill Women's Center, 26

China.

    See One child policy

Choices Women's Medical Center, 38,
        44-45, 124-25

Chu, Jim, 87

Colorado, 126, 171, 177

Cicero, Marcus Tullius, 103

Civil disobedience, 30, 141-42

Civil War, 104

Clinton, Hillary, 137

Collins, John and Adelaide, 20, 34

Colson, Chuck, 11

Contraception, 3, 12, 91, 108

    alleged reason for abortion decrease,
        136-37

    health risks, 167

    See also Pill

Cooke, Terence Cardinal, 149

declares October "Respect for Life
        Month," 172

Courage, 35

Crisis pregnancy centers, 137-38

Croatia, 82

Cuomo, Mario, 35

Daily, Bishop Thomas, 35-38, 50, 124,
        143, 174-75

Darwin, Charles, 91

Diaz, Rose, 63

Dear, Robert, 177

DiMarzio, Bishop Nicholas, vii

Divine Providence, 108, 110

Divorce, 108

Dixon, Beth, 129, 132

DNA, 139

Doe v. Bolton, 6, 97

Donovan, SV, Mother Mary Agnes,
        vii, 83

Drake, James Harlan, 177

Draper Report, 92-93

Dred Scott Decision, 105

Driscoll, Margaret, 165

Drollinger, Frank, 111, 138

Ehrlich, Paul, 90

Eisenhower, Dwight D., 91-92

Ernst, Siegfried, 7-8

Escobedo, MD, Bolivar, 141

Euthanasia, 103

Ex-communication, 98-101

Expectant Mother Care, 139

Fasting.

  See Mortification

Faugno, Emily, 165

Feminism (radical), 91-92

Fetuscope, 139

First Amendment, 118, 121, 133, 144

Fisher, Dietmar, 88

Foreign aid, 91

Forgiveness, 55-56, 67

Forsyth v. Nationalist Movement, 118

Forty Days for Life, 86

Francis, Pope, 94

Franciscan Friars of the Renewal, 34, 174

Freed, Kathryn, 126, 134

Freedom of Access to Clinic Entrances Act, 127, 142, 176

Frozen zones, 124-34

Gag rule, 125-34

Gandhi, Mahatma, 103-104

Garda, Peter, 119, 121

Garijo, Peter, 84

George, Francis Cardinal, xi-xii, 43

Germany, 130

Giuliani, Rudy, 124-25

Gonzales v. Carhart, 176

Goodnow, Dan, x, 86

Gray, Nellie, 25

Griffin, Michael, 140, 175

Griswold v. Connecticut, 21

Groeschel, C.F.R., Benedict, 30, 34, 38

Gunn, MD, Michael, 140, 175

Guttmacher, Alan, 137

Hahn, Scott, 8

Hatch, Orin, 12

Helpers of God's Precious Infants

  budget of, 14

  chapters in the USA, 49

  contribution to the pro-life cause, 145

  current situation, 135-36

  donations to, 14

  effectiveness of, 39, 44-51, 141

  element of sacrifice (in Helpers' success), 49-51

  first large prayer vigil, 175

  founding of, 20, 29-32, 35-36, 117

  fundraising efforts of, 13

  growth of, 32, 48 (overseas)

  growing pains, 32

handouts, 64-68 and Appendix B

hardiness of, 14

Helpers Prayer Book, 78

newsletters, 79

police-protection of, 32

prayer vigils of, 32-33, 69-75

silence of Helpers counselors, 33

sponsorship of Mahony prayer

    vigil, 43

standing at Calvary, 56-57

tactics on the ground, 64-68 and

    Appendix A

trials of, 14, 50

uniqueness of, 12, 49-60, 138,

    145-46

Henry, OFM, Terence, 9

Hering, Wolfgang, 8-9

Hill, Paul, 140, 176

Hobbes, Thomas, 90

Holtzman, Elizabeth, 118-19

Homosexuality, 35, 38, 82, 95-96,

    109, 176

Humanae Vitae, 3, 10, 92, 171

Human Life Amendment, 106-107

Human Life International, 9-10, 41,

    137-38

Hungary, 8, 82

Hyde Amendment, 23-24, 172

Ikpa, Rev. Emmanuel Ray, 84-86

Immaculate Conception Seminary, 16

INTRO 465A, 125-34

Jefferson, Mildred, 27

John Paul II, Pope, 136, 147 173

Johnson, Lyndon, 93

King, Rev. Martin Luther, 107

Kissling, Frances, 72

Kopp, James, 141, 176

Lambeth Conference, 3

Lambs of Christ, 175-77

Law, Bernard Cardinal, 143 ,176

Lejeune, Jerome, 14

Levy, MD, Michael, 129-30, 132

Lisante, Rev. James, 26

Loschin, Beth, 127

Madsen v. Women's Health Center, 176

Magnanimity, 58-60

Mahony, Roger Cardinal, 43

Maloney, Florence, vii, 58

Malthus, Parson Thomas, 90

March for Life, 47

Marino, Mike, 63

Marx, O.S.B., Fr. Paul, 9, 41

Mawn, John, 25

McCorvey, Norma, 6-7

McDonald, Detective Steven, 59-60, 120

Marks, O.P., Sr. Maria Veritas, vii

Marx, Karl, 90

Mary (Mother of Jesus), 31-32

Mary of the Precious Blood, a.p.b., vii

Media bias, 96, 114

Mercy.

    Spiritual works of, 81

    See also Forgiveness; Magnanimity

Missionaries of Charity, 147-48

Monastery of the Precious Blood, vii, xiii-xiv, 39-41

Monck, Francis Xavier, 129, 132

Moore, Eileen, 34

Moore, Frances, 20, 34

Moore, Kevin, vii

Moore, Philip, 89

Moore, Susan, vii

Mortification.

    fasting, 54-55, 145

Mosher, Steven, 137

Mother Angelica, 49-50

Mother Teresa, 147-48

Murphy, Daniel, 109

Nathanson, Bernard, 6, 11, 25, 56, 104, 136, 140, 174

conversion of, 25, 56

producer of *Silent Scream*, 173

National Conference of Catholic Bishops, 98-101

    launches National Right to Life Committee, 171

National Organization of Women, 11, 120 124

National Right to Life Committee, 171

National Security Study Memorandum #200, 93

Natural Family Planning, 21

Natural Law, 102, 110

New Evangelization, 36

New Jersey, 34

New York City, 101

New York City Board of Education, 27-28

New York City Clinic Access Law, 176

New York City Council, 34, 123-28, 176-77

New York State.

    and abortion, 22, 172

    P-Cap program, 122

New York Times, 114

New Zealand, 114

Nixon, Richard M., 92-93

Nobel Peace Prize, 147, 169-70

Obama, Barack, 24

Obergefell v. Hodges, 4

O'Brien, Cornelius, 123-24

O'Connell, Kathleen, 34, 118, 120-24, 127

O'Connor, John Cardinal, 44, 69-75, 83, 124, 175

O'Dea, Maureen, 63

Ogle, Rev. Sean, vii

One child policy, 4, 84

Operation Rescue, 12, 25-26, 29-30, 142, 174-75

Pataki, George, 130

Paul VI, Pope, 3, 8, 21-22

Paverman, Lester, 120

Pavone, Francis, 175

Peiro, Pintor, 84

Pensacola, 29, 173-74

Pill, 21, 91 167, 171

   See also Contraception

Pius XI, Pope.

   Casti Connubii, 3

Planned Parenthood, 10, 43, 61-62, 91, 120, 124, 177

   See also Sanger, Margaret

Police protection, 32, 38, 43, 118, 120-21, 126-27, 134

Pouillon, James, 177

Prayer.

   first prayer at abortuaries, 173

   importance of, 51-54

   power of, 77, 145

   vigils, 32-33

Priests for Life, 13, 175

Pro-choice tactics, 37-38, 50, 69-72, 89, 107, 119, 129-30, 132, 176

Pro-life movement.

   drawing card for non-Catholics, 7-8

   history of, chapter 1

   progress of, 47 (see also: Abortion, decline of)

Putin, Vladimir, 83

Rachel's Helpers, 58

Rachel's Vineyard 58

Reilly, Monsignor Philip J., vii

   address to the World Congress for Life (2010), 90-93

   and blacks, 17

   arrest record, 27, 38-39

   as a "no-namer," 148-49

   athletic prowess of, 16, 18

birth and early years, chapter 2

campaign against legalization of abortion in New York State, 22

campaign against sex education in the schools, 27-28

character of, xiii-xiv, 13, 146-47

cheerfulness of, 114-16

concern for street counselors, 68

contribution to the pro-life cause, ix-x, 145, 147

cosmopolitan breadth of, 7-8, 82-83

courage of, 50, 88-89

declines to found a new religious order, 35-36

defense against charges of incitement to violence, 143-44

devotion to Benediction, 33

direction of 1992 Prayer Vigil led by Cardinal O'Connor, 69-75

economy of expression, 95-96

founding of the Helpers, 29-32

his travels, 48-49

honors received, 147

humility of, xiii-xiv, 49-50

involvement with Operation Rescue, 25, 174

leadership of, 20-21

leaves Cathedral Prep, 40

legal knowledge, 117-18

loneliness and isolation of, 146-48

loyalty to priestly vows and to the Magisterium, 149

views on: abortion, 96-101; fasting, 54-55; church scandal, 110-11; church-state relations, 101-102; contraception, 92, 108-110; Divine Providence, 108, 110, 112-13; ex-communication (of pro-choice Catholic politicians), 98-101; God's mercy, 55-58; the Helpers Mission, Appendix A; Natural Law, 102; US moral decline, 108-109.

optimism of, 110-16

participation in Hundred Mile Walk, 26

prohibition of casual chatter in front of aborturaries, 33

proposal for homiletic reform,
    93-94
rapport with non-Catholics, 7-8, 58
sense of humor, 114-16
skill at the art of comparison,
    104-105
skills: as public speaker, 78; scholar,
    20, 103; street counselor, ix,
    xiii; teacher, 14, 18-20, 77-
    94, 95-96
struggle with cancer, xiii
tactics as a street counselor, 66-68
temporal wiliness, chapter 5
trials of, xiii, 50-51
use of Scripture, 36, 82
vocation of, 15-16
versatility of, 20-21, 24-25
withholding of taxes, 23
Rigali, Justin Cardinal, 43
Right to Life Committee, 43
Rockefeller, Nelson, 22
Roe v. Wade, xii, 4, 22, 24, 96-97
Roeder, Scott, 177
Rogers, Will, 89
Rosary, 31, 33, 38
    power of, 51-52, 71
Rothar, C.S.J., Sr. Dorothy, 13, 122

Rousseau, Jean Jacques, 90
RU 486, 136-37
Ryan, Ada, 25
Ryan, Ed, 115
Ryan, John, 12
Sacrifice, 145-46
Saint Anthony, 74-76
Saint Stanislaus Kostka, 15-16
Saint Teresa's Parish, 18-20
Saint Thomas More Parish, 17-18
Salvi III, John, 140-41, 143, 176
Sanger, Margaret, 91-92
Scheidler, Joseph, 10-11, 86-87
Schenck v. Pro-Life Network, 176
Schindler, Oscar, 147
Science, 139
Seamless garment theory, 35
Shannon, Shelley, 175
Sheen, Bishop Fulton J., 108-109
Silent Scream, 173
Simon, Julian, 90
Singer, Peter, 5
Sisters Adorers of the Precious Blood,
    53-54
Sisters of Life, vii, 175
Sit-ins, 141-42, 145
    first sit-ins, 172-73

Slattery, Chris, 139

Slavery, 104

Slepian, MD, Barnett 141, 176

Sodomy.

   See Homosexuality

Sonogram, 139-40

Sorokin, Pitirim, 7

Stockett, Joseph, 29

Supreme Court, 105, 118

   rulings on abortion, 5, 11, 21, 23,

      47, 126, 173, 175-76

Sweeney, Rev. Kevin, vii

Téglásy, Imre, 87

Teresa of Calcutta.

   See Mother Teresa

Terry, Randall, 11-12, 25, 29-30,

      174-75

The Tablet, 37, 135, 177

TLC Clinic, 46

Tiller, George, 142-43, 175, 177

Trump, Donald, 137

Turnarounds, 44-46, 52, 63, 68, 86-87

Ulrich, Georgene and Matt, 86

Ultrasound, 139-40

United Nations, 21-22, 93 (aid

      program)

Unwin, I. D., 7

Vacile, Sr. Lucie Marie, SV, 83

Vierling, Catherine, 83-84

Vatican II, 36

Vaughan, Bishop Austin, 30, 38, 174

Vienna, 88-89

Violence, 29, 140-45, 172

Wallenburg, Raoul, 147

Warren, James, 127-28

Washburne, Larry, 23

Washington, George, 111

Weslin, Rev. Norman, 177

We Want to Teach, We Want to Be

      Taught, 93-94

Wilson, Malcolm, 22

With Christ for Life, 49

World Congress for Life, 90-93

Wrath of Angels, 136-37

Zevallos, Hector, 142

ABOUT THE AUTHOR

Holding a Ph.D. degree in history from the University of Michigan, Frederick Marks is the author of close to seventy articles, along with ten books, most recently *The Gift of Pain* (2012), *Think and Believe* (2012), *A Catholic Handbook for Engaged and Newly Married Couples* (2014), and *Confessions of a Catholic Street Evangelist* (2017). He has also appeared as a guest on EWTN's "Book Mark" and "Sunday Night Prime."

Made in the USA
Middletown, DE
27 January 2020